Mel Bay Presents

UNDERSTANDIN DADGAD
FOR FINGERSTYLE GUITAR

by Doug Young

1 2 3 4 5 6 7 8 9 0

Visit us on the Web at www.melbay.com — E-mail us at email@melbay.com

CD CONTENTS

1. Example 1 - Tuning and Tuning [01:24]
2. Example 5 [00:18]
3. Example 6 [00:27]
4. Example 8 [00:13]
5. Example 9 [00:19]
6. Example 10 [00:16]
7. Example 11 [00:16]
8. Example 12 [00:17]
9. Example 13 [00:16]
10. Example 14 [00:17]
11. Example 15 [00:32]
12. Example 16 [00:41]
13. Example 17 [00:19]
14. Example 18 [00:18]
15. Example 19 [00:34]
16. Example 21 [00:15]
17. Example 23 [00:18]
18. Example 24 [01:05]
19. Example 30 [00:11]
20. Example 31 [00:31]
21. Example 42 [00:28]
22. Example 44 [00:30]
23. Example 47 [00:18]
24. Example 48 [00:27]
25. Example 55 [00:19]
26. Example 56 [00:15]
27. Example 57 [00:47]
28. Example 65 [00:26]
29. Example 67 [00:25]
30. Example 74 [00:16]
31. Example 75 [00:28]
32. Example 76 [00:07]
33. Example 77 [00:13]
34. Example 78 - Blues For Big Mo [03:07]

35. Example 81 [00:13]
36. Example 82 [00:10]
37. Example 83 [00:14]
38. Example 84 [00:13]
39. Example 86 [00:17]
40. Example 87 [00:16]
41. Example 88 - Reverie [01:02]
42. Example 89 [00:17]
43. Example 90 [00:17]
44. Example 91 [00:11]
45. Example 92 [00:35]
46. Example 96 [00:17]
47. Example 97 [00:12]
48. Example 98 [00:20]
49. Example 99 [00:14]
50. Example 100 [00:18]
51. Example 101 [00:17]
52. Example 102 [00:10]
53. Example 103 [00:07]
54. Example 104 [00:14]
55. Example 105 [00:14]
56. Example 106 - Nuff Said [03:12]
57. Example 109 [00:29]
58. Example 113 [00:37]
59. Example 114 [00:19]
60. Example 115 [00:13]
61. Example 116 [00:16]
62. Example 117 [00:27]
63. Example 119 [00:11]
64. Example 120 [00:23]
65. Example 122 [01:05]
66. Example 137 [00:22]
67. Example 143 [00:25]
68. Example 147 [00:24]

69. Examples 148-156 [02:03]
70. Example 159 [00:25]
71. Example 160 [01:05]
72. Example 174 [00:13]
73. Example 175 [00:19]
74. Example 176 [00:44]
75. Example 177 [00:13]
76. Example 178 [00:12]
77. Example 179 [02:16]
78. Example 180 [00:21]
79. Example 181 [00:16]
80. Example 182 [00:58]
81. Example 183 [00:13]
82. Example 184 [00:11]
83. Example 185 – My Old Kentucky Home [00:58]
84. Example 186 [00:17]
85. Example 187 [00:13]
86. Example 188 - Twinkle, Twinkle Little Star [00:51]
87. Example 189 [00:30]
88. Example 190 [00:14]
89. Example 191 [00:55]
90. Example 192 [00:18]
91. Example 193 [00:18]
92. Example 194 - Oh Susanna [00:46]
93. Example 195 [00:18]
94. Example 196 [00:15]
95. Example 197 - Greensleeves [02:00]
96. Example 198 [00:17]
97. Example 199 [00:14]
98. Example 200 - Swing Low Sweet Chariot [01:09]

Many people helped make this book a reality with their suggestions, early reviews, and encouragement. Special thanks to Tim Alexander, Mike England, Bill Hammond, Jim "Jet" Jarrell, Tom Young, my wife Teri, and of course William Bay, Ken Huxel, Delia Kreftmeyer, Julie Price, and the rest of the staff at Mel Bay.

CONTENTS

INTRODUCTION

DADGAD is an alternate tuning for guitar that has become so popular among acoustic guitarists that some call it "the other standard tuning." The name DADGAD comes from the notes to which the guitar is tuned: D-A-D-G-A-D, instead of E-A-D-G-B-E, as in standard tuning. Most people credit the English guitarist Davey Graham, who started using DADGAD in the 1960's, with developing the tuning. Since then, a wide range of acoustic guitarists, from fingerstyle players like Pierre Bensusan to rock guitarists like Jimmy Page, have adopted DADGAD.

The goal of this book is to show you how to start exploring the many benefits DADGAD has to offer. We will discover the tricks and techniques that make DADGAD fun for the performer and exciting for the listener. We will see how to play chords that sound richer and fuller (or at least different from those you probably use in standard tuning) and also see how to play some things that are difficult, if not impossible, to play in standard tuning. Of course, we'll also discover how to create the harp-like sound that many people associate with DADGAD. But most importantly, we will see how to get around the fretboard and play any chord or melody in any key as readily as in standard tuning, while adding DADGAD's unique character.

I'd like to acknowledge the many guitarists whose explorations of DADGAD have influenced both my music and my understanding of the tuning. As you start your own exploration, you may find it inspirational to check out the music of Pierre Bensusan, Peppino D'Agostino, Alex de Grassi, Laurence Juber, Pat Kirtley, Phil Keaggy, Tony McManus, Al Petteway, John Renbourn, Martin Simpson, John Sherman, Doug Smith, and many others who have used DADGAD for some or all of their music.

TUNING IN DADGAD

There are several ways to approach tuning your guitar to DADGAD. Track 1 on the CD that accompanies this book provides the tuning pitches shown in Example 1. You can also use an electronic tuner, of course.

TRACK 1

EX 1. TUNING NOTES IN DADGAD

TUNING TO DADGAD FROM STANDARD TUNING

If you are starting from standard tuning, simply lower your first, second, and sixth strings one whole step:

◆ Play the fourth string. Now play the sixth string and lower it until it sounds an octave below the fourth string.
◆ Play the fourth string. Now lower your first string until it sounds an octave above the fourth string.
◆ Play the fifth string. Now lower your second string until it sounds an octave above the fifth string.

TUNING BY MATCHING ADJACENT STRINGS

You can also tune by matching pitches of adjacent strings, as shown in Example 2. This approach is similar to the basic tuning method you probably know for standard tuning, but with some adjustments for the altered strings in DADGAD. Tune your sixth string to a D using a piano or other reference pitch. Then:

◆ Match the sixth string, seventh fret, to the open fifth string.
◆ Match the fifth string, fifth fret, to the open fourth string.
◆ Match the fourth string, fifth fret, to the open third string.
◆ Match the third string, second fret, to the open second string.
◆ Match the second string, fifth fret, to the open first string.

EX 2. TUNING BY MATCHING ADJACENT STRINGS

TUNING USING HARMONICS

Another technique uses harmonics. When two notes are out of tune, they create a distinctive beat pattern, and harmonics tend to make these beats easier to hear. The further apart the notes, the faster the beats. When the beats slow and finally disappear, the two notes are in tune. You can also minimize cumulative errors by always comparing each new string with a single reference string. Here's one process that uses harmonics to tune all strings to one common string:

♦ Make sure the fourth string is tuned to the desired pitch. For the rest of this process, do not change the fourth string.
♦ Compare the fourth string, twelfth fret harmonic with the open first string. Adjust the first string, if necessary.
♦ Compare the open fourth string with the sixth string, twelfth fret harmonic. Adjust the sixth string, if necessary.
♦ Compare the fretted note on the fourth string, seventh fret with the twelfth fret harmonic on the fifth string. You may find it easier to play the harmonic on the fifth string first, then fret the fourth string at the seventh fret. Be sure to adjust the fifth string, not the fourth.
♦ Compare the fourth string, twelfth fret harmonic with the third string, seventh fret. Adjust the third string, if needed.
♦ Compare the fourth string, twelfth fret harmonic with the fretted note on the second string, fifth fret. Adjust the second string.

EX 3. TUNING USING HARMONICS

SANITY CHECKS

Regardless of which tuning technique you use, there are some additional sanity checks you can use to make sure everything is correct. For example:

♦ Compare the notes on the fifth string, twelfth fret harmonic and the open second string.
♦ Play a chord by fretting the third string, second fret, and listen to see how it sounds.
♦ Play a chord by fretting the second string, fifth fret, and the third string, seventh fret.
♦ Once you are familiar with the sound of DADGAD, playing a twelfth fret harmonic across all six strings should give you a good idea of whether or not you are in tune.

EX 4. TUNING SANITY CHECKS

HOW TO USE THIS BOOK

This book presents a hands-on approach to DADGAD. You will get the best results if you read it with your guitar in hand. Play the examples, and create your own variations. DADGAD is a fun tuning to explore, so feel free to follow your instincts and change or expand the written examples whenever the inspiration strikes.

The book makes a few assumptions about your background and knowledge of the guitar:

♦ You should be comfortable playing simple fingerstyle pieces that have independent bass lines, melodies and moving voices. This generally requires playing with your thumb and two or three fingers on your picking hand.

♦ You should be able to read tablature and understand chord diagrams. The ability to read standard notation is not required, although it is always helpful.

♦ You should be familiar with standard tuning and know common chords.

♦ You should be comfortable with fundamental guitar techniques, including hammer-ons, pull-offs, and slides.

CD TRACKS

You can hear many of the examples in this book on the accompanying CD. Look for the CD Track markers before each tab example to identify the corresponding track.

PAGE LAYOUT

This book is arranged as a series of topics. In most cases, a pair of facing pages work together to explore a specific topic. Some topics extend to more than two pages, and occasionally a short topic can be contained within a single page. But, as a rule of thumb, you can think of each pair of facing pages as a unit.

TABLATURE

All music in this book is presented in both standard notation and tablature. Unless otherwise noted, all tablature in this book is in DADGAD. In a few rare cases, when we need to refer to standard tuning, the tablature indicates the tuning at the beginning of the staff.

CHORD SYMBOLS

Chord symbols in this book provide suggested fingerings at the top of the chord grid below the chord name. For example, the chord symbol below is a Gadd9. The chord can be played using the third finger at the fifth fret of the sixth string and the second finger at the fourth fret of the third string. The first, second, and fourth strings are played open, while the fifth string is not played.

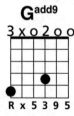

The line at the bottom of the chord symbol indicates the function of the note on each string. For example, in the above chord, the note on the sixth string is the root of the G chord. The fourth and first strings are the fifth of the chord, the third string provides the major third, and the second string is the ninth.

GETTING STARTED

In this chapter, we are going to discover how easy it is to get started with DADGAD. For the examples on the next few pages, you only need to use one finger of your fretting hand! The goal of this chapter is just to get your feet wet, and to discover a few of the interesting sounds you can create with DADGAD. So grab your guitar, get tuned to DADGAD, and dive in.

WHAT YOU'LL LEARN IN THIS CHAPTER

BASIC CHORDS

We'll explore some very simple chords that allow you to get started right away. You only need three chords to play many tunes, and we'll start by learning some easy ways to play these chords in the key of D. You can use these chords to accompany yourself or others, or use them as the basis of instrumental arrangements.

SIMPLE MELODIES

We'll look at a way to play melodies in DADGAD that leverages the open strings to provide the accompaniment, while playing the melody on the third string. This technique allows you to create the sound that many people associate with DADGAD quickly and easily.

ONE WAY TO IMPROVISE IN DADGAD

DADGAD is a wonderful tuning for improvisation. By learning the location of some key notes, it is easy to create melodies "on the fly."

SCALE PATTERNS

Many scale patterns are easier in DADGAD than standard tuning. We'll look at a few of the simplest major and minor scale patterns and explore ways to create melodies and simple arrangements using these scales.

THREE EASY CHORDS

A great way to get started with any new tuning is to find the basic chords you need to play in one or more keys. You can play many simple folk, rock, or pop tunes with just three chords: the I, IV, and V chords of any key. Eventually, you'll want to learn these chords in all keys, but to get started, let's explore one key, the key of D.

BASIC DADGAD CHORDS IN THE KEY OF D

In the key of D, the I, IV, and V chords are D, G, and A7. There are many ways to play these chords in DADGAD, but the chord diagrams below show the simplest way to play a version of each of these chords. Each chord uses only one finger on your fretting hand. You can strum these chords, or use them in fingerpicking patterns. Avoid the first and sixth strings on the A7 chord for now.

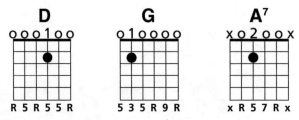

When you play these chord shapes, you may notice that they have a slightly different sound than the D, G, and A chords you know from standard tuning. One of the characteristics of DADGAD is that it is easy to introduce extra notes into chords that change their character. These enhanced chords sound good, and can still function the same way as the more basic chords. To be technically correct:

♦ The D chord used here is a D5, a chord that has only the root and fifth in the chord. It is neither major nor minor, because the chord has no third.

♦ The G chord is a Gadd9/D, because the lowest note is a D, and the A from the second string is the ninth note of the G scale.

♦ The A7 chord has no third. You can also include the open first string, which would make this chord an A11.

In any case, you can use these chords in almost any situation where you would use D, G, and A7. Once you are comfortable with these chords, try to make up some interesting patterns using them, or try to use them as accompaniment for a song.

THEORY: ROMAN NUMERAL CHORD NAMES

It is convenient to identify chords relative to a key, using Roman Numerals like I, IV, and V. These numbers simply refer to the chords built on the first, fourth, and fifth step of a scale. For example, in the key of C, the notes of a major scale are C, D, E, F, G, A, B. So the I chord is a C, the IV chord is an F, and the V chord is a G. The I and IV chords are always major. The V chord is usually a dominant seventh chord, so the V chord in the key of C would be G7. In the key of F, the major scale is F, G, A, B♭, C, D, E, so the I, IV and V chords would be F, B♭, and C7.

It is useful to think about chords as Roman Numerals rather than just by name because the relative numbers allow you to quickly transpose to different keys. Another musician may say, "The progresssion's I, IV, I, V then back to I. Let's play it in G." If you can remember, or figure out the I, IV, and V chords, you can play immediately in any key.

There are also chords that correspond to the other notes of the scale. The chords associated with the second, third, and sixth steps of the scale are all minor, and are usually written using lowercase Roman Numerals. So in C, the ii chord is Dm, the iii chord is Em, and the vi chord is Am. These six chords, the I, ii, iii, IV, V, and vi are the most commonly used chords in any key.

Example 5 outlines the notes of each of these chords in an arpeggio. Notice how the additional notes in these chords create a unique sound.

TRACK 2

EX 5. ARPEGGIOS WITH BASIC CHORDS

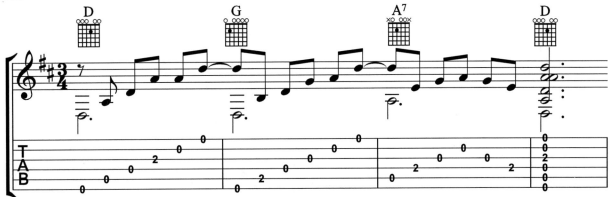

Example 6 demonstrates an alternating bass picking pattern using these chords in a typical chord progression. Play steady quarter notes with your thumb, following the chord progression. For the D chord, the bass alternates between the sixth and fourth strings. For G, alternate between the fifth and fourth strings, or fifth and sixth strings. For A, the root note is on the fifth string, and you can alternate with the fretted note on the fourth string. The treble notes are a bit syncopated and fall between the bass notes. You can experiment with different picking patterns, of course. This is just one possible pattern.

TRACK 3

EX 6. FINGERPICKING WITH BASIC CHORDS

PLAYING SIMPLE MELODIES

DADGAD offers an easy, but effective way to play simple melodies along with a full accompaniment. You can play a melody on the third string, and use the remaining open strings to provide a background harmony. This technique is great for "noodling" and exploring the DADGAD sound. In this section we'll see how to use this approach to make up your own melodies.

Let's start by looking at a D major scale pattern played on the third string, shown in Example 7. You can let the open sixth string ring as you play the notes on the third string, starting on the seventh fret. This pattern starts on the seventh fret, and moves up the D scale to the twelfth fret, then back down to the open third string, before ending at the starting point on the seventh fret.

EX 7. D MAJOR SCALE ON THE THIRD STRING

Once you are comfortable with this scale pattern, you can use the notes in the scale to play melodies. Example 8 demonstrates this idea using the melody to the children's tune, *Frere Jacques*. The melody is accompanied by an alternating bass on the fourth and sixth strings, and by the first or second open strings. When playing this pattern, focus on the third string notes, which define the melody. The other notes provide a "wash" of sound behind the melody, so play them quietly to allow the melody to stand out.

TRACK 4

EX 8. FRERE JACQUES USING A D MAJOR SCALE PATTERN

Let's try another example. Example 9 is in 6/8 time, and alternates the top two open strings with a moving line on the third string, over a sustained bass. Notice that this example moves between a D bass and an A bass (in measures 3 and 4, and again in measure 6). The bass line implies simple chord changes, which tends to relieve the predictability of the constant D bass in the earlier examples. Again, focus on the melody notes on the third string, letting the other notes fill in behind the melody.

EX 9. COMBINING THIRD STRING NOTES WITH OPEN STRINGS

TRY THIS:

1. Pick a simple melody you know - a folk tune, for example - and try to play it on the third string, using the techniques discussed in this section.

2. Make up a melody of your own, using the D major scale on the third string.

THEORY: MAJOR SCALES

Major scales are sequences of notes that follow a specific pattern of whole steps and half steps. On the guitar, a half step (H) is the distance of 1 fret, while a whole step (W) is two frets. The pattern of steps between notes of a major scale is always the same. Look at the intervals between the notes of the C major scale as an example:

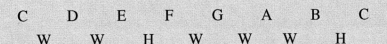

C		D		E		F		G		A		B		C
	W		W		H		W		W		W		H	

Using frets instead of whole/half steps, the pattern of frets between notes of a major scale is:

$$2\ 2\ 1\ 2\ 2\ 2\ 1$$

So, in a C major scale, there is a whole step (two frets) between C and D, as well as D and E. Then there's a half step between E and F. F to G is a whole step, as is G to A and A to B. Finally, B to C is a half step. Once you memorize this pattern, you can play a major scale on a single string starting on any note, even if you don't know the names of the notes. Try it: just pick a note on any string, and play the note, then the note two frets up, then two more frets up, then one, and so on.

It may help to memorize this pattern by breaking it down into two halves. The pattern is 2-2-1, then 2-2-2-1. You might want to play the first four notes, up and down: Root-2-2-1, then back down 1-2-2-Root, in reverse.

Notice that as long as you stay on one string, it doesn't matter what tuning you are in. The same pattern always applies and you can pick out a major scale in any tuning. You won't want to be limited to playing melodies on one string, but the pattern is helpful when you need to find a chord or the notes that make up chords, which we'll get into later. If you pick a note and go up, 2-2-1, the note you land on is the root of the IV chord. Move up two more frets and you have the root of the V chord.

IMPROVISING WITH THIRD STRING MELODIES

The approach of playing melodies on the third string against a background of open DADGAD strings is a great tool for improvising, especially in the key of D. Improvisation often appears to be a mysterious process, but it doesn't have to be. If you've ever picked up the guitar and just let your fingers wander, discovering interesting sounds, you have improvised. Your improvisations can sound more focused and more deliberate, if you have some idea what certain notes will sound like before you play them. DADGAD makes it extremely easy to try one type of improvisation that is almost guaranteed to sound good.

The approach is to play bass notes on the open fourth, fifth, and sixth strings, while playing a melody entirely on the third string. The top two open strings can also be added to provide some harmony. By limiting yourself to playing melodies on the third string, while using the remaining open strings as accompaniment, it is very easy to create a rich, full sound that sounds convincingly as if you know what you're doing! You can play virtually any note on the third string, and not sound wrong, as long as you play with conviction and a sense of direction.

The key is to identify a few target notes on the third string. These are notes that will sound "right" most of the time. Once you become familiar with the sound of these target notes, and can predict how they will sound, you can experiment with any other notes on the third string to make up your own melodies. Just remember to come back to the target notes now and then.

D MAJOR TARGET NOTES

Here are the most important target notes on the third string in the key of D major:

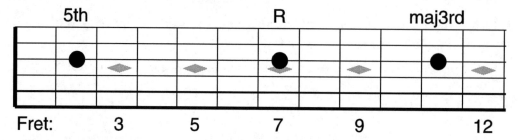

The seventh fret: This is a D, the root in the key of D. You can always land on this target and sound at rest, so this is a good place to start or end a phrase. You can think of it as your "home base" as you play in the key of D. Example 10 demonstrates a simple alternating bass, combined with open first and second strings, and the third string, seventh fret. This example uses a hammer-on from the open third string, which adds some interest to the line.

THEORY: INTERVALS

Terms like *third* and *fifth* refer to the distance between two notes. In a key, we can think of them as steps of a scale, relative to a root. For example, the D major scale consists of the notes: D, E, F♯, G, A, B, C♯, and D. E is the second note of this scale, so the distance from D to E is known as a *second*. G is the fourth note of the scale, so the interval between D and G is a *fourth*. It is also common to modify these intervals. For example, if we lower the E to an E♭, the resulting interval is known as a *minor second*. The interval between D and F♯ is a *major third*, while the distance from D to F natural is a *minor third*.

So, for example, what is the *sixth* of C? Count up the C scale, C, D, E, F, G, A. The notes C and A form an interval of a sixth. What is the *minor seventh* of C? Count up, C, D, E, F, G, A, B. The seventh note is a B, which is a *major seventh*. The minor seventh would be one half step lower, or B♭.

Although there are seven steps of the scale, intervals can go higher, typically up to a *thirteenth*. The interval between two notes that are an octave plus a second apart, is called a *ninth*, because the notes are nine steps apart. An *eleventh* consists of the same note names as a fourth, but are an additional octave apart. Similarly, an interval of a thirteenth will involve the same named notes as a sixth, but the notes are an additional octave apart. For example, the interval between a C and the A above it is a sixth. The interval between a C and the A an octave higher is a thirteenth.

EX 10. PICKING PATTERN IN D MAJOR, ROOT TARGET

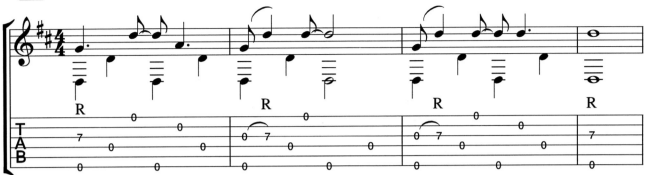

The second fret. This is an A, which is the fifth in the key of D. This is also a very neutral sounding note, and you can also think of it as another "home base." Notice that this position is the same as the simple D chord we learned at the beginning of this chapter. Example 11 shows the same pattern as in Example 10, but uses the second fret as the main target.

EX 11. PICKING PATTERN IN D MAJOR, FIFTH TARGET

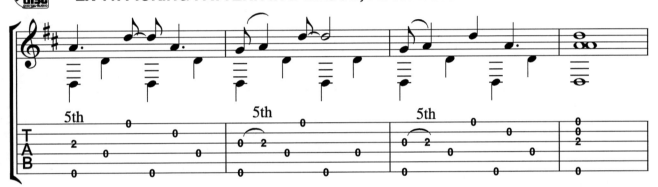

The eleventh fret. The eleventh fret is an F♯, the major third in the key of D. Example 12 demonstrates the use of the F♯ on the eleventh fret (first note in the second measure).

EX 12. D MAJOR ROOT AND THIRD TARGETS

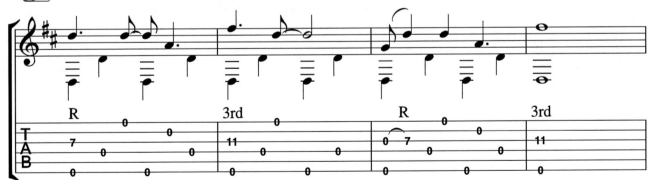

15

IMPROVISING IN OTHER KEYS

You can create different sounds by selecting another set of targets for your melodies or improvisations. Let's look at two possibilities, the keys of D minor and D mixolydian.

D MINOR TARGET NOTES

Here are the most important target notes on the third string for the key of D minor:

♦ **The seventh fret**. This is a D, the root in the key of D. The root is the same whether you are playing in D major or D minor.

♦ **The second fret**. This is an A, which is the fifth in the key of D. This target is also the same in major or minor.

♦ **The tenth fret**. The tenth fret is an F natural, the minor third in the key of D minor. Example 13 combines the root target note with the F at the tenth fret (the first note in the second measure).

♦ **The fifth fret**. The C natural at the fifth fret is the lowered seventh in the key of D. You can actually use either the C♯ or C in the key of D minor, but the sound of the C is probably the most common.

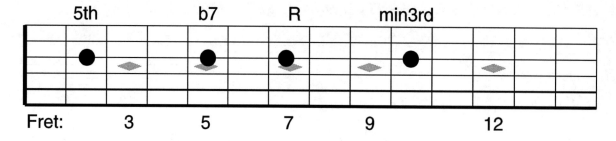

Example 13 demonstrates a picking pattern that uses the D minor target notes.

TRACK 9

EX 13. D MINOR PATTERN

THEORY: MINOR SCALES

Like major scales, minor scales follow a specific pattern of whole steps and half steps. The pattern of intervals between steps of a minor scale is:

$$W\ H\ W\ W\ H\ W\ W$$

Or, in terms of frets:

$$2\ 1\ 2\ 2\ 1\ 2\ 2$$

Once you memorize this pattern, you can play a minor scale on a single string starting on any note. There are other types of minor scales that we will explore later.

16

D MIXOLYDIAN TARGET NOTES

The D mixolydian or D7 scale is similar to the D major scale, but has a lowered seventh. The third string target notes for D mixolydian are:

- ♦ **The seventh fret**. The root.
- ♦ **The second fret**. The fifth in the key of D.
- ♦ **The eleventh fret**. The eleventh fret is an F♯, the major third in the key of D.
- ♦ **The fifth fret**. The C natural at the fifth fret is the lowered seventh in the key of D.

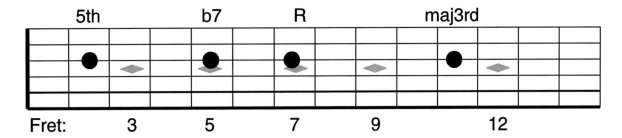

Example 14 demonstrates a picking pattern that uses the D mixolydian target notes.

TRACK 10

EX 14. D MIXOLYDIAN PATTERN

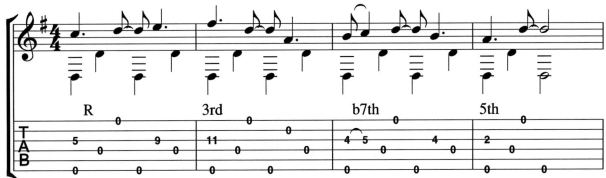

MPROVISATION EXAMPLES

Let's look at a couple of slightly longer examples that demonstrate the technique of improvising a melody on the third string. Example 15 is in the key of D minor and uses 6/8 time. Try damping the bass slightly with your palm and keeping a steady groove as you play the melody line.

EX 15. D MINOR IMPROVISATION EXAMPLE

A MIXOLYDIAN EXAMPLE

Example 16 demonstrates a melody based on the D mixolydian scale. The first four bars use several non-target notes. The first target note, the lowered seventh, sets up a feeling of tension, which is maintained by the notes in the next two bars. These non-target notes lead to the second fret target (the fifth in the key of D) the first time through, and lead to the seventh fret target (the root) the second time. The second section uses the eleventh fret target note to establish a strong major sound, which is carried through the rest of the piece.

TRACK 12

EX 16. D MIXOLYDIAN IMPROVISATION EXAMPLE

Now that you've seen these examples and taken the time to get the target notes in your head, try improvising on your own, or composing your own pieces using these ideas.

Incidently, this same basic approach works on other strings as well. For example, you might try playing melodies on the fourth string while using the remaining open strings as a background.

LEARNING MORE CHORDS

So far in this chapter, everything we've played has required only one finger at a time on the fretting hand, yet we've discovered many useful sounds. Now let's move things up a level, and see what we can do if we use two fingers! We'll begin by expanding our chord vocabulary a bit. You could just look at a big chart of chords, and learn to finger them, but it's more useful to learn how to figure out chords you need on your own. So, this section presents a small set of chords, and discusses ways to find and construct different fingerings for the chords we need.

D MAJOR CHORDS

The first D chord we learned was neither major nor minor, and contained only D's and A's, the root and the fifth. If we add a major third, we will be able to play a true D major chord. Below, on the left, is one D major chord, which simply adds an F♯ on the fourth fret of the fourth string to the shape we learned earlier. This chord has all three notes of a D major triad: D, F♯, and A. There are no extra notes present, so this is a simple D major chord, similar to the first position D chord you probably know in standard tuning.

The fact that the first, fourth, and sixth strings in DADGAD are all Ds is very useful. We'll explore ways to exploit this feature in much more detail later in this book, but for now just realize that any note you can play on one of these strings can also be played on the same fret on the other strings. The note will simply be in a different octave. We can use this information to find two other fingerings for a D major chord, by moving the note on the fourth string to the sixth string, fourth fret, or the first string, fourth fret, as seen in the middle, and right, below.

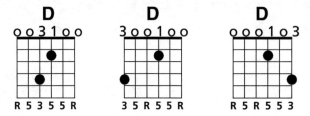

D MINOR CHORDS

Adding an F natural, the lowered third, to the original D shape produces a D minor chord. And, just as with the D major, we can immediately find three D minor fingerings in DADGAD, by playing an F on the third fret of the first, fourth, or sixth strings.

G MAJOR CHORDS

The G chord we learned at the beginning of this chapter was a G triad with a D in the bass. What if we want a G chord with a G in the bass? The lowest G available in DADGAD is on the fifth fret of the sixth string. Adding that note produces the chord on the left, below.

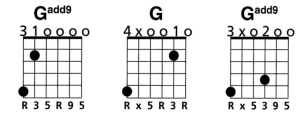

You may find this fingering a bit awkward. Fortunately, it's easy to find some simpler fingerings. Just as you can move notes between the various D strings in DADGAD, you can also move notes between A strings. Moving the note on the second fret of the fifth string over to the second fret, second string, creates the middle G chord, above. This chord is a true G major, consisting of only the notes G, B, and D. The third, B, is the note on the second fret of the second string.

This chord shape is also quite useful, but the fingering is still a bit of a stretch. Another possibility is to move the B, the note on the second string, over to the third string. In DADGAD, any note on the second string can also be played on the third string, two frets higher. The resulting chord is actually a Gm add9 but you can use it nearly anywhere you would play a Gm.

G MINOR CHORD

To create a G minor chord, we simply need to lower the B, which is the major third of G, to a B flat. This is possible, but not very practical with the first two G major chord fingerings above, but it is easy to modify the version on the right. Just lower the note on the third string down to the third fret. The resulting chord is actually a Gm add9, but can be used nearly anywhere a Gm can be used.

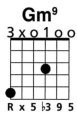

A7 CHORDS

Finally, let's look at some more chord shapes for A. The A7 chord we learned at the beginning of the chapter had no third, so like the basic D chord, it was neither major nor minor. The major third of A is a C♯, which can be found on the fourth fret of the second string. Adding a C♯ to the A chord shape we learned earlier, suggests several new chords. The chord shape on the right has no third, but it does allow you to play the top string without the suspended fourth sound.

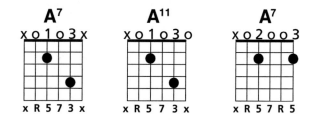

A MINOR CHORDS

You can create an A minor chord shape by adding a C natural, the minor third of A to the basic A chord shape.

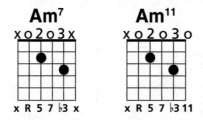

APPLYING THE NEW CHORDS

Let's look at a few examples that use some of these new chord forms. Example 17 uses the D and G major chords, along with the new A11 chord.

TRACK 13

EX 17. USING TWO-FINGER MAJOR CHORDS

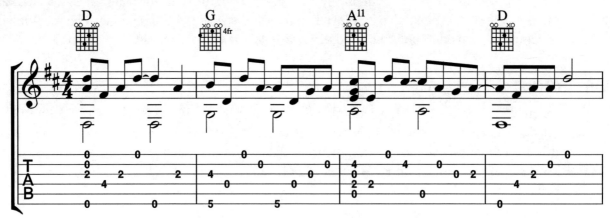

Example 18 transforms this same idea into a minor key, using some of the minor chords we've just learned.

TRACK 14

EX 18. USING TWO-FINGER MINOR CHORDS

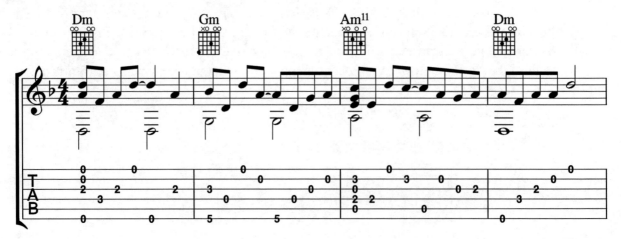

Example 19 is a longer fingerstyle example that uses many of the D, G, and A7 chords we've just learned. The chord diagrams show which chord fingering to use at any given time. The arrangement does not always use all the notes in each chord, but you can visualize, and in most cases finger, the complete chord shape. Seeing the chord shapes in your mind can help you to under stand the structure of the tune better than if you just try to think about the individual notes.

The only tricky part about this example is knowing when to shift from one chord shape to the next. The melody sometimes anticipates the chord change. Also notice that in some places, like the last few notes of measure 2, the piece lets the chord drop and simply uses the open strings during a transition from one chord to the next. Because the open strings all belong to a D major scale, these notes tend to fit anywhere, and this technique contributes to the typical DADGAD sound.

TRACK 15

EX 19. APPLYING NEW CHORD FORMS

23

SIMPLE SCALE PATTERNS

So far, we've explored ways to play scales and melodies using just the third string. There's also an extremely easy way to play scales and melodies horizontally in DADGAD, across the strings.

MAJOR SCALE PATTERNS

The scale pattern in Example 20 forms a D major scale from the low D on the sixth string to the F♯ on the fourth fret of the first string. With one exception, this pattern consists entirely of notes on the second and fourth frets and open strings. The pattern duplicates two notes between the third and second strings. Scales and scale patterns are useful for playing melodies and this pattern makes it easy to pick out melodies as well as to improvise. As long as you use only the open strings and the notes in the second and fourth frets, you can play in the key of D and never play a wrong note.

EX 20. MAJOR SCALE PATTERN ON TWO FRETS

Example 21 uses the notes from this scale pattern in a typical melodic line, played over an alternating bass.

TRACK 16

EX 21. MELODIC EXAMPLE USING TWO-FRET MAJOR SCALE PATTERN

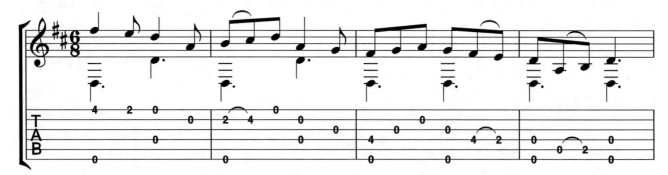

If you have learned scale patterns in standard tuning, you will certainly appreciate how easy this is. To play melodies in DADGAD, you need only use two fingers, and the same two frets across the fretboard! There are no complex shapes that change as you move between strings. As with the third string scale patterns, it would be a good idea to use this pattern to play some melodies you know. You can also try to improvise, or just make up a melody, using this scale pattern.

MINOR SCALE PATTERNS

You may be surprised to discover that you can also play a scale pattern using the open strings combined with the notes on the third and fifth frets. Unlike the second and fourth fret pattern, this pattern contains the notes of the D minor scale. This pattern skips a few notes of the complete D minor scale, and a few notes are repeated. But, as with the major scale pattern, you will be able to pick out many minor melodies using only these notes, and you should find it easy to improvise in D minor by selecting notes from this pattern.

Example 22 shows how to play this pattern on the third and fifth frets.

EX 22. MINOR SCALE PATTERN ON TWO FRETS

To appreciate how useful these two simple patterns are, play something using the notes on the second and fourth frets. Then move it to a minor key, simply by sliding your hand up one fret and repeating the same pattern. Example 23 demonstrates this idea. The fingerings in Example 23 are identical to those in Example 21, except that the pattern is played one fret higher, creating a minor version of the melody.

TRACK 17

EX 23. MELODIC EXAMPLE USING TWO-FRET MINOR SCALE PATTERN

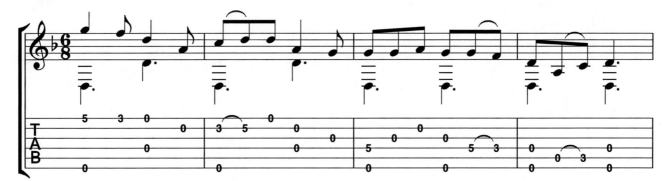

TRY THIS:

1. Pick a simple melody you know, a folk tune, for example, and try to play it using the scales demonstrated here.
2. There are also similar patterns available between frets 4 and 7, 5 and 7, 7 and 9, 7 and 10, and 10 and 12. Experiment with these and see what types of sounds thcsc patterns create. Take note of whether these shapes sound minor or major and how the fretted notes interact with the open strings.

PUTTING IT ALL TOGETHER

We've covered a lot of ground in this introduction, although none of the examples use more than two fingers and three basic chords. One of the exciting things about DADGAD is the way the tuning allows you to create music with less effort than you might expect. Because you can play things that sound good with less physical effort, you can concentrate on playing musically.

Let's conclude this chapter with an example that combines most of the ideas and techniques we've seen so far. Example 24 is a short piece in the key of D major that combines many of the chords introduced in this chapter with melodies that use the open strings as well as the notes on the second and fourth frets.

As you try this piece, notice that you can think of the melody (the top notes of the tune) as coming entirely out of the second and fourth fret scale pattern from Example 20. You can also think of the melody as being formed around chord shapes, with connecting passing notes. The chord shapes are shown above the tablature. In some cases, these chords correspond exactly to what is played in the tab. At other times, the chord forms represent what you might visualize while you are playing, but you don't necessarily have to play the entire chord.

This example also uses more hammer-ons and pull-offs than earlier examples. Although hammer-ons and pull-offs are fundamental guitar techniques that are useful in any tuning, DADGAD seems to provide many additional opportunities to use them effectively.

The first eight bars of Example 24 introduce the main theme, which is in the key of D major. The second set of eight bars forms a bridge, which moves to G briefly, but quickly returns to D major. After the bridge, the piece reprises the melody one last time.

TRACK 18

EX 24. COMBINING SIMPLE SCALES AND CHORDS

LEVERAGING STANDARD TUNING

In the next few chapters, we're going to discover some simple ways to get your bearings and begin to understand how to use the entire fretboard in DADGAD. Once you learn a few simple rules, you should be able to find some form of almost any chord, and be able to play scales in any key in DADGAD. Once you can locate these chords and scales, you can think of them as signposts that guide you as you explore the unique sounds that DADGAD has to offer.

You may have already noticed that in DADGAD, the third, fourth and fifth strings are tuned to exactly the same pitches as they are in standard tuning. This can be quite helpful when learning DADGAD, because it lets you apply many things you already know from standard tuning directly to DADGAD. In this chapter, you'll learn how to leverage your knowledge of chords and scales in standard tuning to understand DADGAD quickly.

When learning to speak another language, you must eventually learn to think in that language to be able to speak fluently. But, you would most likely start by translating a few common words and phrases you know from your native language. We can apply the same concept to learning a new tuning, like DADGAD. In this chapter, we'll focus on translating chords, scales and licks we already know from standard tuning into DADGAD. Later, we'll start to see how to think directly in DADGAD.

WHAT YOU'LL LEARN IN THIS CHAPTER

HOW TO CONVERT STANDARD TUNING CHORD SHAPES TO DADGAD

We'll see how to translate chord shapes in standard tuning into equivalent chords in DADGAD. In addition, we'll also see how to use your geometric understanding of the fretboard in standard tuning as a framework for playing in DADGAD.

HOW TO CONVERT STANDARD TUNING SCALES TO DADGAD

We'll explore the relationship between scales in standard tuning and DADGAD, and see how to convert some simple scales and licks to DADGAD.

USING STANDARD TUNING CHORD SHAPES IN DADGAD

Let's start by looking at a few chords. A simple first position E chord is one of the first chords guitarists learn in standard tuning. You can use the same chord shape in DADGAD, as long as you play only the third, fourth, and fifth strings. Compare the following chord shapes.

Std Tuning	DADGAD
E	**E**
o 2 3 1 o o	x 2 3 1 x x
R 5 R 3 5 R	x 5 R 3 x x

The shape on the left is a normal E major chord in standard tuning. The shape on the right uses only three strings; the open strings are not played. This chord still sounds like an E major chord and can be played in standard tuning or DADGAD.

Almost any standard tuning chord shape that sounds good when you play only strings three, four, and five can also be used in DADGAD. For example, compare the following two C chord shapes:

Std Tuning	DADGAD
C	**C**
x 3 2 o 1 o	x 3 2 o x x
x R 3 5 R 3	x R 3 5 x x

The chord on the left is the normal first position C chord in standard tuning. The partial chord on the right is also a C chord in both standard tuning and in DADGAD.

Now look at a first position A chord. The shape below on the left is one you know in standard tuning. Playing just the third through fifth strings produces a shape that can be used in DADGAD.

Std Tuning	DADGAD
A	**A**
x o 1 2 3 o	x o 1 2 x x
x R 5 R 3 5	x R 5 R x x

This A chord form can be fingered as a moveable chord shape that rock guitarists know as a "power chord." A power chord is played on three strings and contains only roots and fifths. Below are a few different power chords that you can play in either standard tuning or DADGAD:

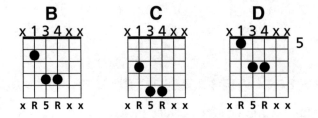

30

You may wonder how it helps to be able to play these partial shapes. What good are chords that only use the three middle strings on the guitar? Well, there are at least four ways to use this information.

1: A QUICK WAY TO PLAY A CHORD

If you are reading a chord chart, or playing with other people while in DADGAD, and encounter a chord you have not played before, you needn't worry. Just grab the shape of the nearest chord you know in standard tuning, and just play the third, fourth, and fifth strings. It may not be the coolest chord that you could find, but it will work, and it won't sound like a wrong note.

2: A BASIC SHAPE TO WHICH YOU CAN ADD OPEN STRINGS

Many of these chords sound good when you add the open first and second strings. For example, the chord on the left below is a partial C chord that can be played in standard tuning or in DADGAD. The chord on the right adds the top two open strings. The two open strings create a C6/9 sound, which is a pretty chord that can be used in place of a regular C major chord.

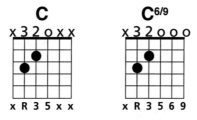

3: A BASIC SHAPE TO WHICH YOU CAN ADD ADDITIONAL FRETTED NOTES

You can start with the basic shape, but add other notes as you see fit. For example, the following DADGAD chords are all extensions of the basic C shape:

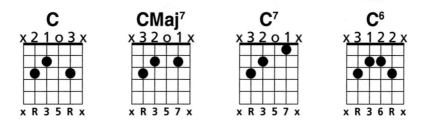

You can visualize in your mind the shape you are already familiar with from standard tuning, and just think of these shapes as variations of the standard tuning shape, which should help you memorize them quickly.

4: A VISUAL FRAMEWORK FROM WHICH TO PLAY SCALES OR MELODIES

Many players learn scale shapes that they associate with chord forms, as a visualization tool. This same principle works in DADGAD, and we can use shapes we know from standard tuning as a way to orient ourselves when playing scales and melodies. We'll take a more in-depth look at scales later on.

CREATING CHORDS BY SHIFTING STRINGS

Now that we've seen how various standard chord shapes can be played on the middle strings in DADGAD, the next step is to realize that the remaining three strings have simply been lowered one whole step, or two frets. Therefore, notes whose locations you know on those strings from standard tuning can be found in DADGAD by moving two frets up to compensate.

For example, consider an Am7 chord. The chord diagram below, on the left, shows one way to finger this chord in standard tuning. To play the same chord in DADGAD, we simply need to move the notes on the top two strings up two frets, as shown on the right:

Std Tuning	DADGAD
Am⁷	**Am⁷**

For some chords, eliminating a few notes may make the chord easier to finger. For example, consider an F chord in standard tuning, as shown on the left, below. To convert this chord shape to DADGAD, move the two top strings and the bottom string up two frets:

Std Tuning	DADGAD
F	**F**

The resulting chord shape is hard to finger, but dropping a few strings creates shapes that are easier to play. The shapes below are reasonable DADGAD fingerings for F.

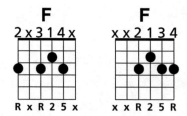

The chord shape below on the left is the familiar standard tuning first position C chord. By raising the notes on the top two strings, we can create the shape needed in DADGAD, as seen in the second chord below. Dropping a few notes creates several easier fingerings.

MOVEABLE CHORD FORMS

By converting chords from standard tuning, we can find a collection of moveable chords in DADGAD very quickly. Moveable chord forms are especially valuable because once you've learned the chord shape, you instantly have as many as twelve chords available.

The F major chord described in the previous section is one moveable chord. From this basic shape, you can play as many different major chords as you can reach on your guitar. For example, here are some major chords, all using the same shape, at different positions on the neck:

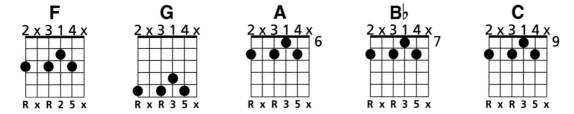

We can also create moveable minor and dominant seventh chords, using the technique of moving the notes in the standard tuning version on the first, second, and sixth strings up two frets. For example, compare the following standard and DADGAD versions of Gm:

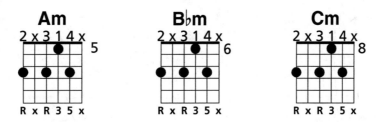

You can move the resulting shape around the fretboard to create any minor chord you like:

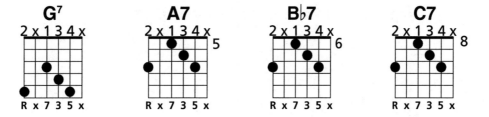

The dominant seventh chord can be handled the same way, producing the following moveable shapes:

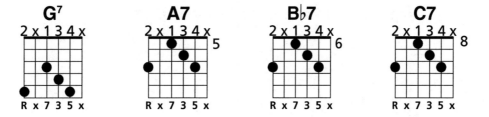

Once you know these three shapes, you can play all twelve major, minor, and dominant seventh chords in DADGAD. These fingerings may not always the most convenient shapes for these chords, but they are a starting point. If you need to play a Bb7 chord in DADGAD, for example, you know where you can grab at least one chord shape that will work.

CONVERTING SCALES FROM STANDARD TO DADGAD

Just as you can apply what you know about chords in standard tuning to DADGAD, you can also leverage the scales you know in standard tuning. Consider the C major scale in standard tuning shown in Example 25.

EX 25. A C MAJOR SCALE IN STANDARD TUNING

This scale runs from C to A, about an octave and a half. In DADGAD, the notes on the third, fourth, and fifth strings will be the same as in standard tuning, but you'll need to shift the notes on the top two strings up by two frets to play the same notes.

The process of shifting notes may be easiest to visualize with a fretboard diagram. Example 26 shows the notes of a C scale in standard tuning as dots on the fretboard. The square markers in this diagram are the root notes of the scale. The notes in the grey boxed area on the top two strings are the notes that must be changed for DADGAD. Just mentally shift those notes up by two frets as shown in the diagram on the right, which produces the same notes in DADGAD.

EX 26. ADJUSTING A C MAJOR SCALE PATTERN FOR DADGAD

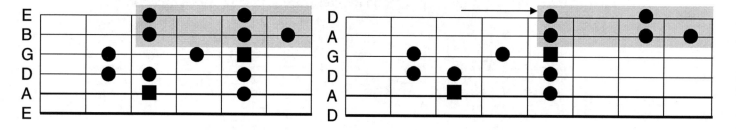

Example 27 shows the shifted C major scale form in tablature form.

EX 27. C MAJOR SCALE IN DADGAD

Later we will discover fingerings that are more convenient, but for now, focus on visualizing how the C scale you may already know can be transformed into a scale in DADGAD.

CREATING BLUES SCALES IN DADGAD

This shifting technique works for any scale. Example 28 shows how you can convert the box shape of a blues scale to DADGAD.

EX 28. ADJUSTING A BLUES SCALE PATTERN FOR DADGAD

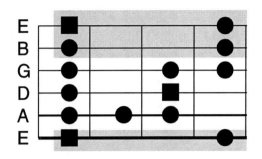 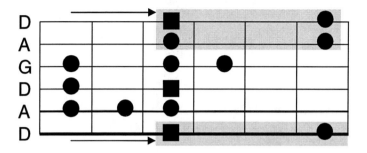

Example 29 shows the tab for an A blues scale in DADGAD, created by shifting the top and bottom strings of the standard tuning pattern.

EX 29. A BLUES SCALE IN DADGAD

Example 30 demonstrates a simple blues lick over a monotonic bass line, in the key of A, using the converted DADGAD blues scale. Notice how the notes of the melody all come from the blues pattern from Example 29. From just listening to this example, you would not necessarily know that it was being played in DADGAD.

TRACK 19

EX 30. BLUES IN DADGAD USING A SHIFTED BLUES SCALE PATTERN

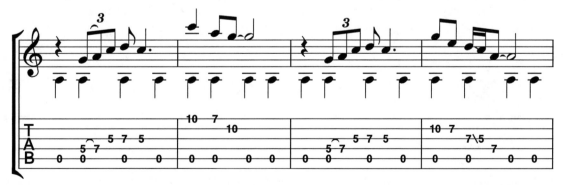

You can use this simple technique to convert any licks you know in standard tuning to DADGAD. For example, many blues licks are played using the top two strings. You can play those same licks in DADGAD, just shift them up two frets. With a little practice, you can quickly translate any of your licks into DADGAD.

THE CAGED SYSTEM

The *CAGED* system is a useful approach to understanding and organizing the fretboard in standard tuning. CAGED is an acronym that stands for five chord shapes, C, A, G, E, and D. The CAGED system can be useful in DADGAD as well as standard tuning.

CAGED IN STANDARD TUNING

Let's start by reviewing how the CAGED system works in standard tuning. There are five basic chord shapes, which correspond to each of the chords in the first position, as shown below.

Each of these shapes can be converted to a moveable shape and used to play any major chord. Here are the moveable forms of these shapes:

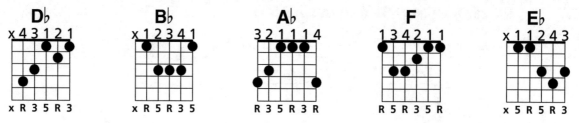

Using these five moveable chord shapes, it is possible to play any chord at five different locations on the fretboard, using the shapes in order, C, A, G, E, D. The five chord sequence covers twelve frets, at which point, the sequence starts over. For example, below are the five places you can play a C chord, starting with a first position C shape. The second way to play a C chord is with an A shape at the third fret. The next C chord uses the G shape at the fifth fret, followed by the E shape at the eighth fret. The last chord in the sequence uses the D shape at the tenth fret.

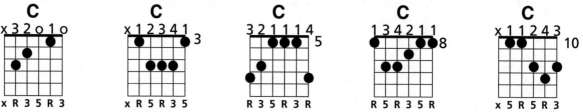

You can apply this pattern to any chord, but you will usually have to loop back to lower positions at some point. For example, look at the following CAGED sequence in F.

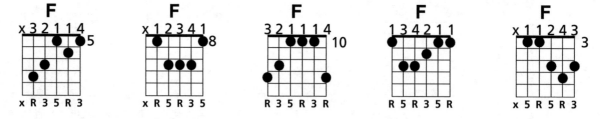

This system is extremely useful as a way to organize the fretboard. Not only does it help you locate any chord in any position, but you can use it to locate scales, arpeggios, and more. If you think of scale patterns as being associated with chord shapes, then they also follow the CAGED system.

CAGED IN DADGAD

Now, let's see how CAGED works in DADGAD. The concept is the same as it is in standard tuning; the shapes are simply changed. Here are the five fundamental first position shapes in DADGAD:

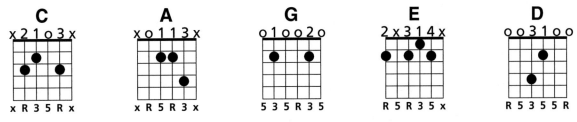

Now let's see how you can play a C major chord in all five positions in DADGAD:

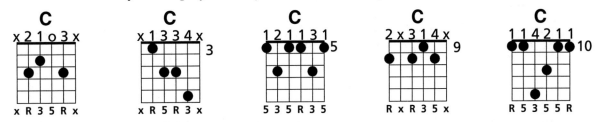

The CAGED concept can also apply to other types of chords. For example, consider the following five minor forms of the CAGED chords:

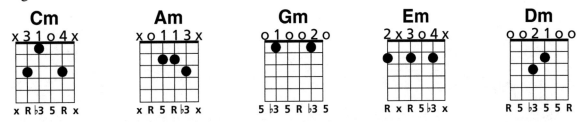

We can use moveable forms of these shapes to play C minor chords in all five positions.

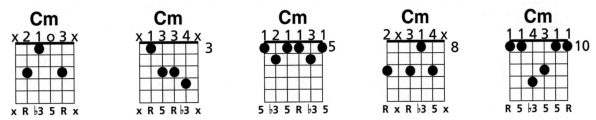

As in standard tuning, the DADGAD forms can be applied to any chord, and the sequence can start anywhere, and moves through the same C,A,G,E,D cycle of forms. Here is an F major chord in all five positions in DADGAD, in CAGED order:

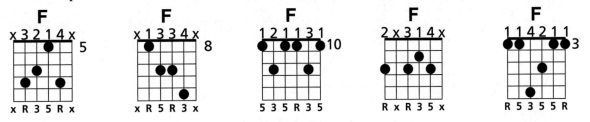

Some of these chord shapes are not very comfortable to play, and few of them take advantage of the musical characteristics of DADGAD. The point is to be able to locate them and use them as musical guideposts for locating notes on the fretboard. We'll explore this in more detail later when we look at scale and arpeggio patterns.

PUTTING IT ALL TOGETHER

Let's finish our discussion of converting from standard tuning to DADGAD with a short example that uses some of the chord shapes we've just learned. Notice that this example, in the key of C, doesn't sound much different than it would sound if you played something similar in standard tuning. However, DADGAD does make a few patterns available, such as the hammer-on from D to E at the beginning of measure two, that would not be as natural in standard tuning.

TRACK 20

EX 31. APPLYING "CONVERTED" CHORDS FROM STANDARD TUNING

INTERVALS AND HARMONY

In this chapter, we'll explore harmony based on intervals as a way of organizing and thinking about the fretboard in DADGAD. An interval is simply the distance between two notes. The word *harmony* can be used in several different ways. Harmony can refer to the sound that comes from playing or singing two similar melody lines in which the notes are some interval apart. People also talk about harmony when they discuss the chord progression, or harmonic structure, of a tune. Intervals actually play a key role in both meanings of the word. Intervals provide a good way to enhance melodies by adding harmony, but can also be useful for creating an accompaniment, or supplying the harmonic structure of a tune, because they are the building blocks of chords.

WHAT YOU'LL LEARN IN THIS CHAPTER

INTERVAL BASICS

It's helpful to understand a bit of the theory behind intervals, including naming conventions and how intervals are used to create harmony. We'll discuss just enough to understand how to apply the ideas in this chapter to concrete examples.

HARMONIZED SCALES USING THIRDS, SIXTHS, AND TENTHS

We'll see how to apply these intervals to harmonized melodies and explore the geometric patterns that can help you memorize scales harmonized in thirds. The intervals of a sixth and a tenth are closely related to thirds, and are also useful for harmonizing melodies. We'll see how to use all of these intervals to harmonize melodies and create arrangements.

HOW TO USE INTERVALS AS SIMPLE CHORD SHAPES

In addition to their role in harmonizing melodies, we'll see how to use intervals as skeletal chord shapes. When used this way, intervals provide a very effective way to understand and organize the fretboard, and to create some very distinctive sounds in DADGAD.

HOW TO USE OCTAVES AND UNISONS

Even simple intervals can be useful tools, and DADGAD provides some unique opportunities to use octaves as well as unisons to create some interesting effects.

INTRODUCING INTERVALS

An interval is simply the distance between two notes. If you count up the notes of a C major scale, C, D, E, F, and so on, D is the second note of the scale, so the interval between C and D is called a second. The interval from C to E is a third, C to F is a fourth, and so on. It's helpful to be able to identify the notes of any scale in terms of the numbered steps of a scale, as shown in Example 32. For example, A is the sixth note of the C scale, so the interval between C and A is a sixth.

INTERVAL NAMES

Most intervals have several forms. For example, the interval between C and D consists of two half-steps, and is known as a *major second*. The distance between C and Db (or C#) is one half step and is called a *minor second*. Example 33 lists most of the possible intervals relative to a single note, C, starting with a *unison*, which is two notes played together, all the way up to a thirteenth, which is two notes thirteen scale steps apart.

Intervals are often a source of confusion because they use seemingly inconsistent naming conventions. Seconds, thirds, sixths, and sevenths are referred to as *major,* indicating the way the intervals normally occur in a major scale, or *minor* if they are lowered. For example, the interval between C and E is a third, specifically a major third, while the interval between C and Eb is a minor third.

However, the interval of a fourth, is referred to as a *perfect fourth*. There is no minor fourth, but you can raise the fourth a half step to create an interval known as an *augmented fourth*. C to F is an example of a perfect fourth, while C to F# would be an augmented fourth. The interval of a fifth is also known as a *perfect fifth*. Like fourths, fifths can be augmented. Fourths and fifths can also be lowered by half a step, in which case they are referred to as *diminished*. You may hear other terms for these intervals. Sometimes a diminished fifth or augmented fourth is called a *flat five*, and an augmented fifth is sometimes called simply a *sharp five* or *raised five*.

Although there are only seven notes in a scale, intervals can extend beyond that. For example, a *ninth* is created by two notes nine steps apart, which is the same as an octave plus a second. The interval of a *tenth* is an octave plus a third. *Elevenths* and *thirteenths* are also common.

The interval names summarized in Example 33 are worth memorizing. Many of them are useful for harmonizing melodies, and you may encounter any or all of them when constructing chords. The intervals we'll be using in this chapter to harmonize melodies are major and minor thirds, sixths and tenths, octaves and unisons (the same note doubled).

HARMONIZED SCALES

Harmonizing melodies is one important application of intervals. For example, we can harmonize a C major scale in thirds by playing each note of the scale along with the note three steps above. Example 34 shows how this works using standard notation. We'll see how to play harmonies on the guitar in the following pages, but for now, just notice how the harmony consists of two parallel scale patterns, three steps apart.

You can harmonize scales and melodies using many different intervals in addition to thirds. For example, Example 35 shows a scale harmonized in fifths. Each note of the C scale is played at the same time as a note five steps above. Example 36 shows a scale harmonized in sixths.

Being able to play scales using various intervals is very helpful, and can make it easier to harmonize melodies. In the rest of this chapter, we'll explore how to find harmonized scales and melodies on the guitar in DADGAD and see how a good understanding of intervals can help unlock the fretboard.

EX 32. NUMBERED NOTES OF A C MAJOR SCALE

EX 33. INTERVAL NAMES

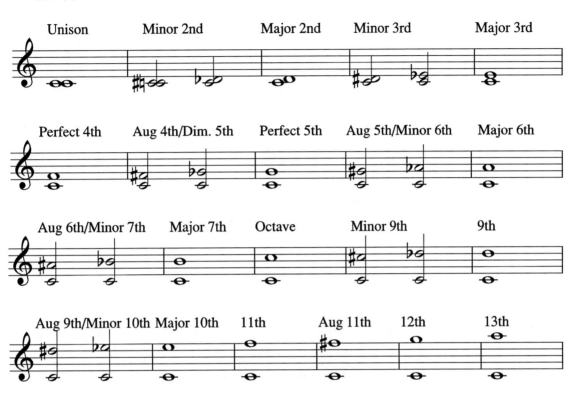

EX 34. C MAJOR SCALE HARMONIZED IN THIRDS

EX 35. C MAJOR SCALE HARMONIZED IN FIFTHS

EX 36. C MAJOR SCALE HARMONIZED IN SIXTHS

HARMONIZING WITH THIRDS

The most common way to add harmony to any melody is to add a parallel line three steps higher than the original melody. This interval is known as a *third*, because the two notes are three steps apart. We'll explore thirds by looking at some scales and scale patterns, and then applying these patterns to some melodies.

Example 37 shows one way to play a C major scale, harmonized in thirds. This scale is played entirely on the top two strings of the guitar. The C major scale is played on the second string, while the notes on the first string follow the scale, three steps higher. You may not be able to play the scale all the way up to the fifteenth fret unless your guitar has a cutaway. Don't worry if you can't play the entire line, the idea is to understand the pattern.

EX 37. C MAJOR SCALE IN THIRDS ON TOP STRINGS

Notice that the notes of the harmonized scale form the following geometric pattern:

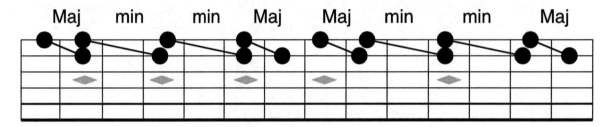

There are two different shapes in the pattern. The first is the major third, where the two notes are one fret apart. The second is a minor third, where the notes are two frets apart. The first pair of notes form a major third, while the second and third steps of the scale are harmonized with minor thirds. The fourth and fifth steps of the scale use major thirds, while the sixth and seventh are harmonized with minor thirds. So the sequence of intervals that make up a major scale harmonized in thirds is always:

Major - minor - minor - Major - Major - minor - minor - Major

Once you memorize this pattern you can play scales or melodies in thirds in any key. Notice that this pattern can be split into two smaller, identical patterns of:

Major - minor - minor - Major

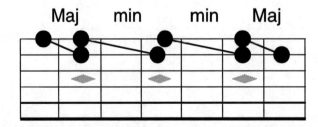

This short segment repeats in each half of the scale. Try playing it forwards and backwards at as many locations of the fretboard as you can. Example 38 demonstrates the C major scale, broken into chunks of four steps, playing both up and down the scale.

EX 38. C MAJOR SCALE HARMONIZED IN THIRDS IN GROUPS OF FOUR

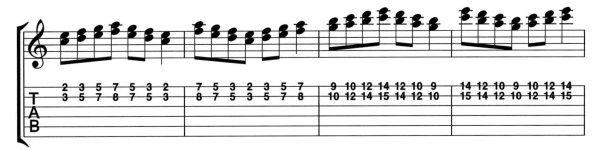

To play melodies using harmonized scales, you need to be able to play the notes in any order. Example 39 shows an example exercise that will help you get used to playing the notes in different orders, and help cement the pattern into your memory.

EX 39. C MAJOR SCALE PATTERN HARMONIZED IN THIRDS

Example 40 demonstrates a harmonized thirds pattern applied to a melody. The example is in the key of D, so the pattern is simply shifted up two frets from the C scale pattern. The example also introduces a bass line below the melody.

EX 40. TWINKLE TWINKLE LITTLE STAR HARMONIZED IN THIRDS

HARMONIZED THIRDS ON THE FOURTH AND FIFTH STRINGS

You can also play harmonized patterns in thirds on other strings. In DADGAD, the fourth and fifth strings have exactly the same notes as the first and second strings, just an octave lower. Therefore, the same pattern of thirds can be played on both the first and second strings and the fourth and fifth strings. Example 41 shows a C major scale on strings four and five.

EX 41. C MAJOR SCALE IN THIRDS ON STRINGS FOUR AND FIVE

This pattern is identical to the pattern on the top strings. Compare the following fretboard diagram with the one on the previous pages. You can play this pattern starting at any point on the fingerboard.

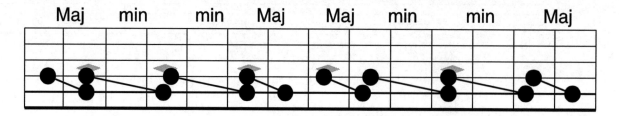

Harmonized thirds on the lower strings can sound very nice when combined with the remaining open strings. Example 42 demonstrates a simple melodic line on the fourth and fifth strings, along with arpeggios on the open first, second and third strings. This example moves the pattern to the key of D, which just slides the pattern from Example 41 up by two frets.

TRACK 21

EX 42. THIRDS ON FOURTH AND FIFTH STRINGS

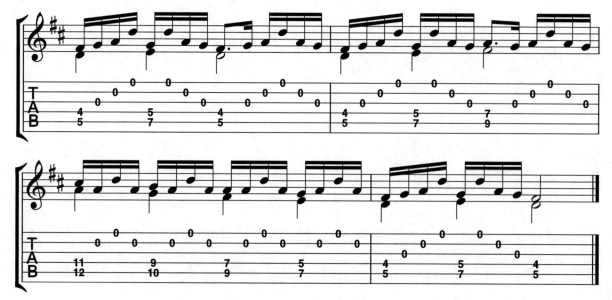

HARMONIZED THIRDS ON THE THIRD AND FOURTH STRINGS

The pattern on the third and fourth strings is especially useful. Example 43 shows a harmonized F major scale on the third and fourth strings. Notice that the geometric shapes of the pattern is the same as the major scale on the first and second strings, but this scale starts on an F.

EX 43. F MAJOR SCALE IN THIRDS ON STRINGS THREE AND FOUR

Although the notes are different, the sequence of shapes is exactly the same. Try this pattern at different places on the fretboard on the third and fourth strings.

Example 44 demonstrates this pattern in a more melodic setting, combining open strings and bass notes with the thirds. Here, the pattern is in the key of D, and descends from the top of the scale.

TRACK 22

EX 44. D MAJOR SCALE PATTERN IN THIRDS ON MIDDLE STRINGS

HARMONIZED THIRDS ON SECOND AND THIRD STRINGS

The pattern on the second and third strings is a bit different. Example 45 shows a harmonized A major scale.

EX 45. A MAJOR SCALE IN THIRDS ON STRINGS TWO AND THREE

The geometric pattern still follows the same pattern of major and minor intervals, but the shapes of the intervals are different from the shapes on the other strings.

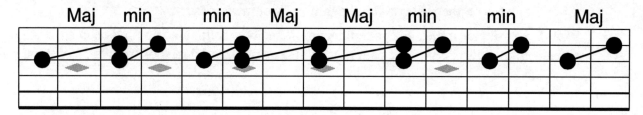

PLAYING THIRDS ACROSS STRINGS

Once you can play these harmonized scales and patterns, you will find many different ways to use them. For one thing, you needn't play them up and down the fretboard as we've been doing. Learning the scales on adjacent pairs of strings is a useful way to learn these patterns, but once you know the shapes, try to find these intervals everywhere you can on the fretboard.

Example 46 shows a melodic pattern in two keys, using fragments of the patterns we've looked at in the same location of the fretboard, moving across strings. The first four bars demonstrates the pattern in the key of C, while next four bars move the same pattern up two frets to the key of D. Try this in other keys as well.

EX 46. PLAYING THIRDS IN ONE POSITION

MORE HARMONIZED THIRDS

One way to get these patterns under your fingers is to apply them in different ways. For example, try the scale pattern in Example 47. This is just a D major scale, harmonized in thirds, primarily on the third and fourth strings. But Example 47 adds a rhythmic bass line and plays the scale using a slightly syncopated pattern that is more fun to play than a straight scale.

TRACK 23

EX 47. A MORE MUSICAL SCALE PATTERN

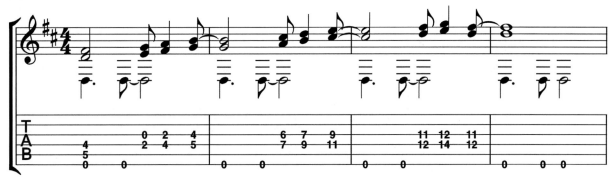

You also don't necessarily need to play entire melodies in harmonized thirds as we've been doing so far. Instead, you can visualize these patterns and use them as targets around which to build melodies, much like the third string target notes we discussed earlier.

Example 48 is a short piece in A minor that uses harmonized thirds at key points in the melody. You can visualize the harmonized thirds as you are playing, treating them as targets around which to place notes that add variety and interest to the melody. In this example, the notes that belong to harmonized thirds patterns are indicated with a star.

TRACK 24

EX 48. USING THIRDS AS TARGETS WITHIN A MELODY

HARMONIZING WITH SIXTHS

We saw earlier that any note that can be played on the fourth string can also be played an octave higher on the first string, and any note that can be played on the fifth string can also be found an octave higher on the second string. Example 49 demonstrates moving the bottom voice in a series of harmonized thirds to a higher octave by changing strings. The result is a series of intervals known as sixths, because the two notes are six scale steps apart. You can think of sixths as just inverted thirds.

EX 49. INVERTING THIRDS TO FORM SIXTHS

Example 50 shows an F major scale, harmonized in sixths, using the first and third strings. The sound is similar to that of harmonized thirds, but a bit more "open" sounding. A scale harmonized in sixths follows the same alternating sequence as thirds.

EX 50. AN F MAJOR SCALE IN SIXTHS

As with thirds, it may be useful to visualize these intervals as a series of geometric shapes. Here are the shapes of the sixths pattern on the first and third strings.

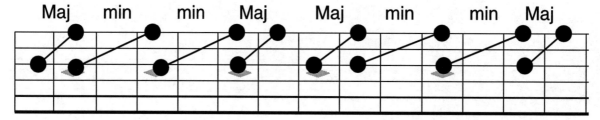

Like thirds, sixths can be played in any key, and are useful for harmonizing melodies. Try Example 51, a familiar tune in the key of A.

EX 51. TWINKLE, TWINKLE, LITTLE STAR IN SIXTHS

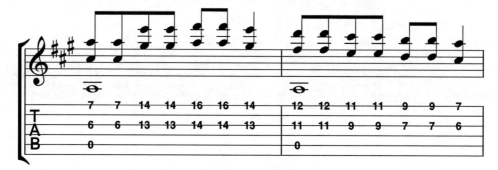

48

SIXTHS ON THE OTHER STRINGS

The pattern of sixths on the second and fourth strings is the same as on the first and third. Here are the geometric shapes:

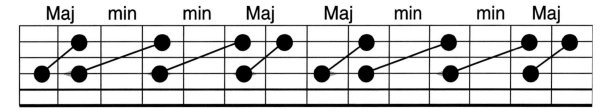

Example 52 shows this pattern applied to a C major scale.

EX 52. C MAJOR SCALE IN SIXTHS

The pattern of shapes is slightly different on the third and fifth strings. The sequence of major, minor, minor, major remains the same, but the shapes associated with these intervals change.

Example 53 shows an A major scale in sixths, using the pattern on the third and fifth strings.

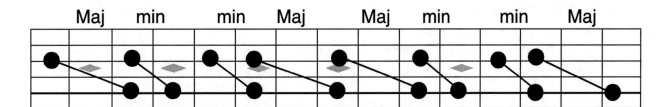

EX 53. A MAJOR SCALE IN SIXTHS

Remember that all of these patterns can be played starting at any point, and that you can break them down into repeating sections of four notes each. Example 54 provides some more practice in the key of A, using two pairs of strings.

EX 54. TWINKLE TWINKLE LITTLE STAR IN SIXTHS

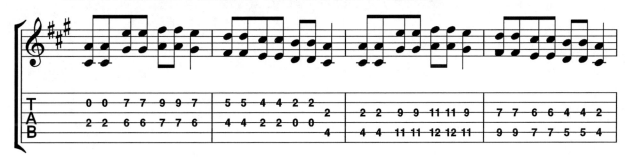

APPLYING SIXTHS

Like harmonized thirds, sixths can be used as a way of thinking about the fretboard and extended to create a fuller sound. For example, just as we can add in open strings when playing lines in harmonized thirds, we can also add open strings when playing with sixths. Example 55 shows one way to combine a simple melody, harmonized in sixths, with the open strings, over a droning bass on the 6th string.

TRACK 25

EX 55. COMBINING SIXTHS WITH OPEN STRINGS

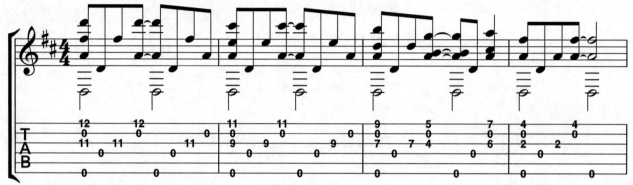

Example 56 combines sixths with open strings and pull-offs, interspersed with a picking pattern that uses open strings.

TRACK 26

EX 56. COMBINING SIXTHS WITH PULL-OFFS AND OPEN STRINGS

USING SIXTHS AS TARGETS

Example 57 is a longer example that combines extensive use of harmonized sixths with some other elements. The first measure is a two-beat pickup that introduces a simple pull-off lick that appears several times in the tune. The second measure uses a D major scale, harmonized in sixths to introduce the main theme.

Notice that throughout the piece, you can usually visualize a harmonized sixth pattern, even when the piece incorporates other elements. For example, measure 3 is an arpeggio based on the shape of a sixth interval on the second and fourth strings.

The bass line uses a syncopated pattern in most measures, with a bass note on the downbeat of each measure, and then again on the upbeat of the second beat of the measure. It helps create a nice groove if you cut off the initial bass note slightly by resting your thumb on the string just before playing the second bass note. You can add a percussive effect if you rest your thumb more forcefully. Listen to the recording to see how this might sound.

EX 57. ARRANGEMENT BASED ON SIXTHS

HARMONIZING WITH TENTHS

The interval of a tenth is similar to a third, but the notes are an additional octave apart. So, a tenth is an octave plus a third. We can find the interval of a tenth on the fretboard by starting with a thirds shape on the top or middle pairs of strings, and simply moving the lower note over to a string an octave below.

Example 58 shows how to move from an interval of a third on the top two strings to a tenth, by moving the note on the second string to the same fret on the fifth string. Next, we see how to move from an interval of a third on the third and fourth strings to a tenth on the third and sixth strings.

EX 58. CONVERTING THIRDS TO TENTHS

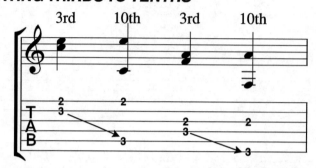

Example 59 demonstrates a C major scale using tenths, played on the first and fifth strings. Notice that tenths form the same pattern of major and minor intervals as thirds:

Major - minor - minor - Major - Major - minor - minor - Major

Once you memorize this pattern, you can play tenths in any key by just shifting positions. As with thirds, and sixths, the pattern can be broken down into identical chunks of four.

EX 59. C MAJOR SCALE IN TENTHS

You can also play tenths using the third and sixth strings, as shown in Example 60. The pattern on the third and sixth strings is the same on the first and fifth strings.

EX 60. F MAJOR SCALE IN TENTHS

TENTHS AS SKELETAL CHORDS

Tenths are extremely useful in DADGAD, because you can view them not only as harmonized scales, but also as skeletal chord shapes. You can think of the bottom note of each interval as the root of a chord, and the upper voice as the third. Example 61 shows a harmonized F major scale with implied chords.

EX 61. F MAJOR SCALE IN TENTHS WITH IMPLIED CHORDS

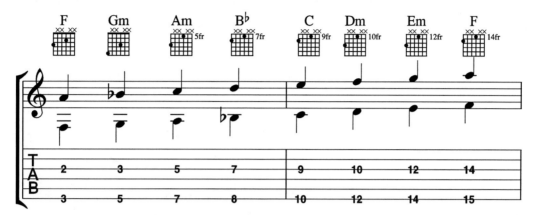

In many cases, it is also possible to add the open strings to these chords to get interesting effects. The open strings add a constant set of tones to each chord, but the open strings interact differently with each chord. Example 62 shows the chords produced by adding the first, second, and fourth open strings to the fretted notes in Example 61.

EX 62. F MAJOR SCALE IN TENTHS WITH OPEN STRINGS

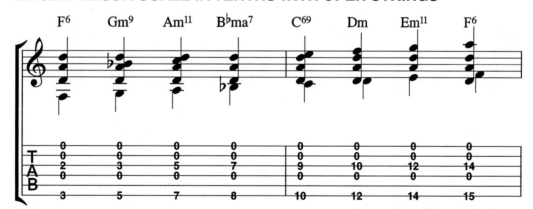

Example 63 shows the basic skeletal chord shapes for major, minor and seventh chords. Starting with a root note on the sixth string, you can add a major tenth above, which acts as a major chord. If you lower the tenth by half a step, the result will sound like a minor chord. Adding a seventh between the root and the tenth will add the seventh sound. These are movable chord forms that can be used anywhere on the fretboard.

EX 63. SKELETAL CHORD SHAPES USING TENTHS

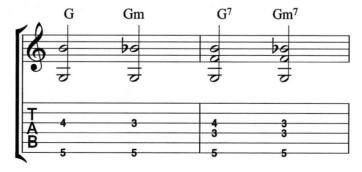

USING TENTHS WITH OPEN STRINGS

We saw how the open strings interact with a harmonized F major scale. You can also explore what happens when adding open strings to each of the movable chord forms in Example 63 at different locations on the fretboard. Example 64 shows a few of the chords created by playing the major tenth interval at various locations, along with some of the open strings.

EX 64. EXTENDING SKELETAL CHORD SHAPES WITH OPEN STRINGS

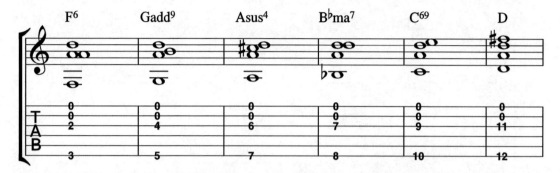

These tenths-based chord forms also work nicely with open strings when used in an arpeggio pattern. Example 65 is in the key of G major and uses tenths as the basis of the harmony as well as the primary melodic line, with the open strings providing a drone.

TRACK 28

EX 65. ARPEGGIOS USING TENTHS AND OPEN STRINGS

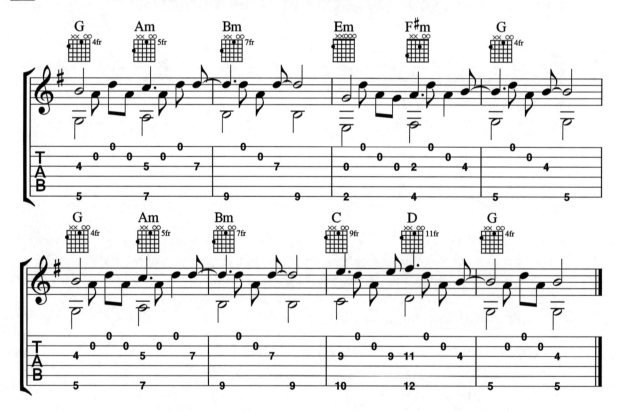

54

UNISONS

A unison is simply the same note doubled, which may not seem very useful at first glance. However, very few single instruments are capable of playing a unison. It's not possible to play two instances of the same note at once on a piano, or a saxophone, for example. Many recordings use multiple players, or multiple takes to double melody lines on instruments like saxophones, vocals, or lead guitar, to create a fat, thick texture. It is possible to play some notes in unison on the guitar, in any tuning. However, because the second and third strings in DADGAD are only a whole tone apart, it is easy to play entire lines as or unisons in DADGAD. Example 66 demonstrates a partial D major scale using doubled notes.

EX 66. PARTIAL SCALE IN UNISONS

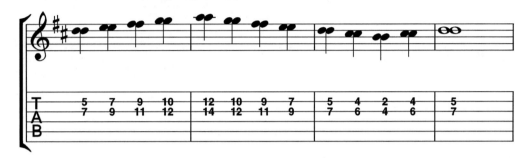

Unisons can create a very striking effect if not overused. Example 67 is an eight-bar example in the key of D minor that demonstrates how unisons might be used in a realistic musical context. Example 67 does not show the unisons in the standard notation, to keep the notation from looking cluttered. The tablature shows the notes that should be played as unisons. Try sliding into some of the unison notes to give them more emphasis.

TRACK 29

EX 67. USING UNISONS IN AN ARRANGEMENT

OCTAVES

Octaves are pairs of notes played eight scale steps apart. Octaves are used in many guitar styles, but they are especially useful in DADGAD because they are easily accessible on three pairs of strings. In DADGAD, the fourth and sixth strings are an octave apart, as are the first and fourth strings. The second and fifth strings, which are both tuned to A, are also an octave apart. On most strings you can add an octave by simply adding a note on the same fret, a few strings over. Example 68 shows a simple ascending D major scale in octaves using the first and fourth D strings.

EX 68. OCTAVES ON FIRST AND FOURTH STRINGS

Example 69 demonstrates an A major scale in octaves, using the second and fifth strings.

EX 69. OCTAVES ON SECOND AND FIFTH STRINGS

You can also play octaves using the fourth and sixth strings. Example 70 shows a two-octave major scale, in octaves, starting on the fourth and sixth strings, and ending on the twelfth fret of the first and fourth strings.

EX 70. D MAJOR SCALE IN OCTAVES

Notice that there is one string between the octaves when you play on the fourth and sixth strings, but you must skip two strings when playing octaves on the second and fifth strings, as well as on the fourth and first strings. Practice picking the lower line in the octaves with your thumb, and also playing both strings using only your fingers, freeing your thumb to play bass notes at the same time.

Although it is common to use octaves in standard tuning, DADGAD supports several techniques that are difficult, if not impossible to do in standard tuning. Example 71 demonstrates using hammer-ons in octaves. The first two bars use hammer-ons from open strings to fretted notes, while the second two bars use hammer-ons from fretted octaves, played by barring with your first finger, to an octave on a higher fret.

EX 71. HAMMER-ONS IN OCTAVES

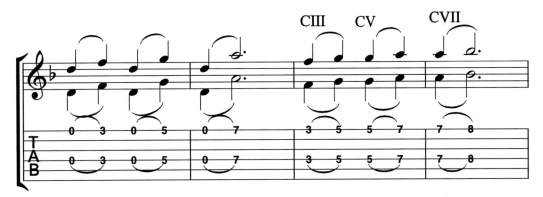

You can also use octaves with pull-offs, either using open strings or fretted notes. Example 72 demonstrates a line that is the opposite of that in Example 71, pulling off from each set of higher notes to the note below. The third and fourth bars are challenging to play, but it can be done.

EX 72. PULL-OFFS IN OCTAVES

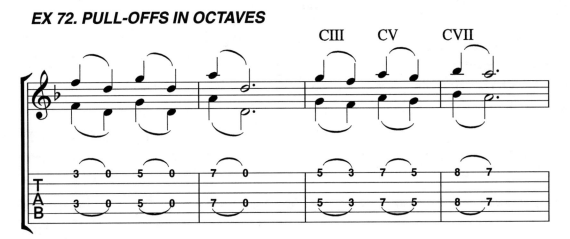

It is also possible to play double octaves, so that the upper and lower voices are two octaves apart, using the first and sixth strings. Example 73 shows a D major scale in double octaves.

EX 73. DOUBLE OCTAVES

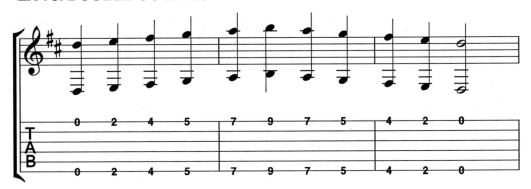

OCTAVE EXAMPLES

Example 74 combines hammer-ons, pull-offs and slides to create a more complex example using octaves. Lines like this are useful for creating dramatic effects, solo breaks, and so on.

EX 74. COMBINING HAMMER-ONS, PULL-OFFS, AND SLIDES

Octaves can also be combined with bass lines. Example 75 shows a simple example that uses the open fifth and sixth strings as the bass, while playing a melody on the upper strings in octaves.

EX 75. OCTAVE MELODY OVER BASS NOTES

PUTTING IT ALL TOGETHER

Let's complete the topic of using intervals with a complete arrangment that uses many of the techniques we've been exploring. Unlike the demonstration examples we've been looking at, real tunes are unlikely to be based entirely on a single technique. Example 78 on the next page, a tune named "Blues for Big Mo," uses a variety of techniques, including octaves, unisons, sixths, thirds, fifths, as well as assorted chord and scale ideas.

The form of "Blues for Big Mo" is ABACBA. The A section is 8 bars long, and uses octaves, with hammer-ons, pull-offs, and slides to create the main theme, as seen in Example 76.

EX 76. BASIC MELODY OF BLUES FOR BIG MO

After the second ending, the B section modulates to a G7. This section uses a more percussive technique, as seen in Example 77. The arrows indicate that these notes are played with the back of the nails, in a downstroke that combines a strum and a percussive hit. Notice the use of unisons in the third and fourth measures (measures 15 and 16 in the full tune on the following pages).

EX 77. BRIDGE SECTION OF BLUES FOR BIG MO

After the B section, the A section is played again, but goes to the fourth ending, which flows into an improvised solo section. You may want to experiment with your own solo in this section. The example solo written here uses many of the harmonized thirds and sixths ideas from this chapter.

After the solo, return to the bridge, the B section, then repeat the A section once before ending at the coda.

Play "Blues for Big Mo" with a blues shuffle, and a bit of a loose, relaxed feel.

EX 78. BLUES FOR BIG MO

TRICKS AND TECHNIQUES

Every tuning, including standard tuning, has certain idiomatic patterns that work particularly well. Finding and taking advantage of these characteristics is one of the things that makes playing the guitar fun. DADGAD has many interesting features that can be exploited to create music that sounds different than most tunes played in standard tuning. In this chapter, we'll explore some of DADGAD's characteristic techniques and "tricks."

WHAT YOU'LL LEARN IN THIS CHAPTER

HARP-LIKE CROSS STRING PATTERNS

The first thing many people think of when you mention DADGAD is the harp-like sound of cascading open strings. We'll explore how to create this effect.

REALLY SIMPLE WAYS TO PLAY CHORDS

We've seen quite a few chords already, but there are some very simple tricks that can be used in DADGAD that allow you to "cheat" and play really simple shapes that work well in many situations, even though they are not entirely correct.

HOW TO USE SHAPE-BASED HARMONY

DADGAD seems to lend itself well to various parallel harmony techniques. We'll explore what this is and how it can be used.

HAMMER-ONS, PULL-OFFS, AND PERCUSSIVE TECHNIQUES

We'll look at how these techniques, which are commonly used in all tunings, can be leveraged in DADGAD.

TEN THINGS YOU CAN'T DO IN STANDARD TUNING

Every tuning has some unique features that allow you to play things that are difficult to play in other tunings. We'll look at a collection of things that you can do in DADGAD that you either can't do, or at least that are more difficult to do, in standard tuning.

CROSS-STRING PATTERNS

Many people associate DADGAD with a harp-like sound. You can create this sound, which comes from playing scales and patterns across the strings, in any tuning, but it does work particularly well in DADGAD. The effect is easy to achieve in DADGAD, in part because of the major second interval between the second and third strings. For example, try the three-note partial scale in Example 79.

EX 79. PARTIAL D MAJOR SCALE

This example places three consecutive scale notes on three different strings. To get the intended effect let all three notes ring. These three notes are the key to the harp sound in DADGAD. Now, try the D major scale in Example 80. This scale sounds no different than it would in standard tuning, because all the notes are played as fretted notes.

EX 80. FRETTED D MAJOR SCALE

Next, try the cross-string version in Example 81. Pay close attention to the fingerings and try to keep all notes ringing as long as possible; shift your fingering only when absolutely. For example, keep the first note ringing until you have to fret the fourth string on the third note. Keep the second note fretted and ringing until you have to move your hand to play the sixth note on the fourth fret of the third string. Example 81 uses the same notes as Example 80, but the sound is quite different.

TRACK 35

EX 81. D MAJOR CROSS-STRING SCALE

SLURS AND CROSS-STRING PATTERNS

You can extend the harp-like sound into longer, more complex lines by adding hammer-ons and pull-offs. Example 82 shows a partial G major scale on the top three strings. The cross-string sound is partially broken by the hammer-on and pull-off on the first string, but the overall effect remains as long as you play the line smoothly. Notice that you do not need to lift your third and fourth fingers. Also keep your second finger down while playing the hammer-on on the first string.

TRACK 36

EX 82. G MAJOR CROSS-STRING PATTERN WITH SLURS

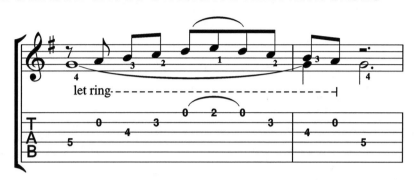

Example 83 demonstrates a similar line starting in A major. This example uses no open strings. The harp effect is created by maintaining your fingering on all notes as long as possible.

TRACK 37

EX 83. CROSS-STRING PATTERN WITHOUT OPEN STRINGS

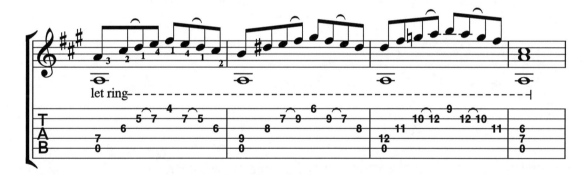

Example 84 is based on the D major scale cross-string pattern, but adds pull-offs, a slide, and a broken scale pattern. Notice how the harp effect grows as the line progresses. By the end of the lick, all six strings should still be ringing.

TRACK 38

EX 84. CROSS-STRING PATTERN WITH SLURS BASED ON A SCALE

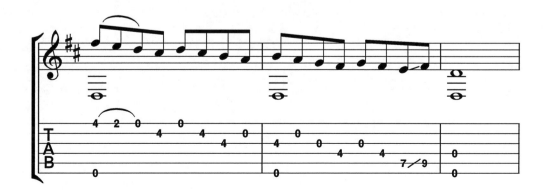

MORE CROSS-STRING PICKING PATTERNS

There are many different ways to exploit the cross-string effect in DADGAD. Example 85 shows a picking pattern using two strings along with your thumb and finger. Pay close attention to the fingerings of both hands and try to keep the first string ringing as you play the second note, and then the second note ringing as you play the third note.

EX 85. CROSS-STRING THREE-FINGER ROLL PATTERN

Once you are comfortable with this pattern, try shifting it across the strings, as shown in Example 86. As you move across the strings, allow the open strings to keep ringing.

TRACK 39

EX 86. EXTENDED CROSS-STRING THREE-FINGER ROLL PATTERN

This pattern works well in many places in DADGAD. Example 87 shows one variation, played on the second and fourth frets. Notice the pull-off at the beginning of the pattern. Other than the pull-off, you can play this pattern with the same fingering pattern used in Example 86.

TRACK 40

EX 87. D MAJOR CROSS-STRING PATTERN

66

Example 88 is the first verse of a tune named *Reverie* that uses both open-string and fretted cross-string patterns. The tune is quite rubato, so play each phrase in a conversational way. The changing time signatures aren't as complicated as they look, they're just a rough indication of the length of the different phrases. Try to keep as many strings ringing as possible throughout the piece.

EX 88. EXAMPLE ARRANGEMENT USING CROSS-STRING TECHNIQUES

Reverie

Doug Young

PARALLEL HARMONY

DADGAD allows you to create some harmonic sounds that are somewhat unusual. One of these is the sound of tight clusters of parallel harmony. The idea is simple: take a shape and move it around the fingerboard, usually over a sustained bass. The result is a jazzy suspended sound, that is somewhat tonally ambiguous. Example 89 demonstrates one simple pattern. Once you're used to the sound, try to create your own licks based on this idea.

TRACK 42

EX 89. USING PARALLEL HARMONY

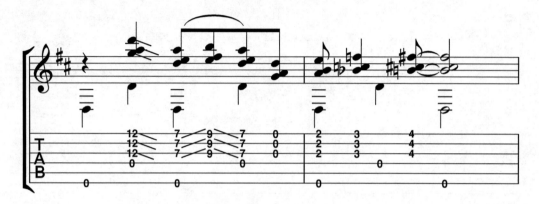

Example 90 combines parallel harmony with pull-offs.

TRACK 43

EX 90. PARALLEL HARMONY WITH PULL-OFFS

Example 91 uses a different shape. Notice all the accidentals and close chord voicings. These close clusters of sound create chords that are difficult to name. The extremely close, dissonant chords would be difficult to achieve in standard tuning.

TRACK 44

EX 91. PARALLEL HARMONY

CHEATER CHORDS

We've explored quite a few chord shapes, and eventually you should be able to play almost any chord you want in DADGAD. But there are times when you just want to play some chords that work without worrying too much about the exact type of chord. You may just need "a G" or "an F". The following two-finger chords sound good and are about as easy as it gets. Each chord simply consists of the root and a fifth on the bottom two strings, with the open strings adding an interesting color above the bass notes. The quality of each chord will be different, depending on the way the open strings interact with the fingered notes.

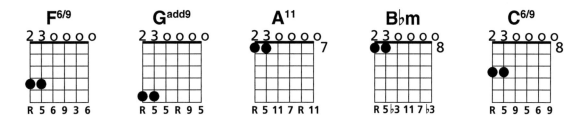

These chord shapes work well for strumming, and can be used to create a ringing, jangly rhythm sound. But they also can be used in fingerstyle arrangements. Example 92 demonstrates both sounds.

TRACK 45

 ### EX 92. TWO-FINGER CHORD EXAMPLE

HARMONICS

Harmonics are an effective guitar technique in any tuning. Because of the geometry of the guitar, harmonics are available in DADGAD at the same frets as in standard tuning. The most common places are the twelfth, seventh, and fifth frets, although there are harmonics available on almost every fret. Of course, in DADGAD, the pitches of these harmonics are different than the pitches found in standard tuning.

Example 93 shows the notes available on the twelfth fret, using harmonics. At the twelfth fret, the pitches produced by the harmonics are exactly the same as they would be if you fretted the notes.

EX 93. TWELFTH FRET HARMONICS

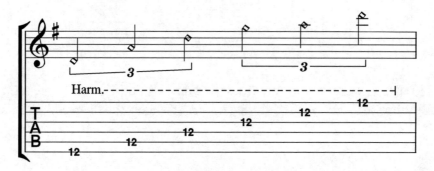

The harmonics at the fifth fret produce the same notes as at the twelfth fret, but an octave higher. The harmonics at the seventh fret are a fifth higher than the twelfth fret harmonics. Example 94 shows these harmonics.

EX 94. FIFTH AND SEVENTH FRET HARMONICS

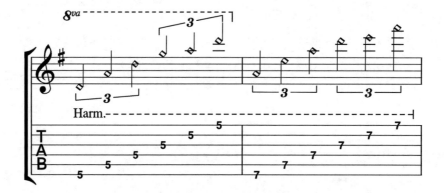

Harmonics at the fourth and ninth frets produce the same notes. It is more difficult to get clean harmonics at these locations, but with practice, it can be done.

EX 95. FOURTH AND NINTH FRET HARMONICS

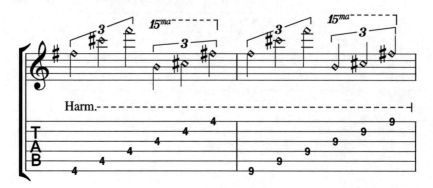

HARMONIC PATTERNS

Harmonics can be used in many different ways. Example 96 is a riff that mimics the parallel harmony we looked at earlier, but uses harmonics.

TRACK 46

EX 96. HARMONICS AND PARALLEL HARMONY

Example 97 shows one way to play a scale using only open string harmonics.

TRACK 47

EX 97. D MAJOR SCALE WITH HARMONICS

Harmonics add a nice color to a fingerpicking pattern, and blend well with the sound of open strings. Example 98 shows one way to use harmonics within a fingerstyle pattern.

TRACK 48

EX 98. HARMONICS INTERSPERSED WITH A FINGERPICKING PATTERN

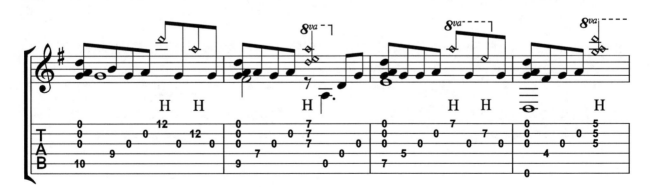

HAMMER-ONS AND PULL-OFFS

DADGAD seems to naturally encourage the use of hammer-ons and pull-offs. Example 99 shows a D major scale pattern that combines a cross-string pattern with both hammer-ons and pull-offs to create a smooth sound.

TRACK 49

EX 99. D MAJOR SCALE WITH HAMMER-ONS AND PULL-OFFS

Example 100 is a pattern based on the third and fifth fret D minor scale pattern we first learned at the beginning of this book.

TRACK 50

EX 100. HAMMER-ON/PULL-OFF PATTERN WITH A D MINOR SCALE

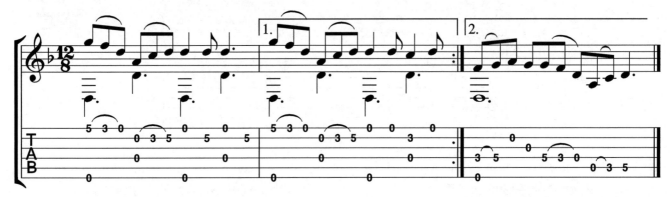

Hammer-ons and pull-offs don't necessarily need to be between adjacent notes of a scale. In DADGAD, hammer-ons and pull-offs work well between open strings and any fretted note, as shown in Example 101.

TRACK 51

EX 101. HAMMER-ONS AND PULL-OFFS WITH NON-ADJACENT NOTES

PERCUSSIVE TECHNIQUES

We could devote an entire book to percussive techniques on the guitar. Example 102 illustrates two similar techniques, a string slap and a slap harmonic, both of which work well in DADGAD. To create a string slap, simply slap the open strings with your non-fretting hand, holding your fingers flat. If you strike exactly at the twelfth fret, you can get a slap harmonic effect. In fact, you can also get this effect by slapping twelve frets higher than any fretted note. You can also get a similar effect by slapping five frets or seven frets above the fretted note. When practicing, try to be as accurate as you can. In actual use, you won't need to worry about hitting specifc strings or frets precisely. Just aim for the intended location and try to get close.

Example 102 uses both of these techniques. The first measure starts with a slap on the open strings. Just hit the strings at any fret position, and aim for the bottom three strings. Then, hammer-on with your fretting hand, and slap the strings at the twelfth fret, aiming for the middle three strings on the first slap, and the upper three strings on the second. The second measure repeats this same pattern. This time, barre at the fifth fret, and create the slap harmonics by aiming at the seventeenth fret, twelve frets above the barred fifth fret.

EX 102. SLAP HARMONIC EXAMPLE

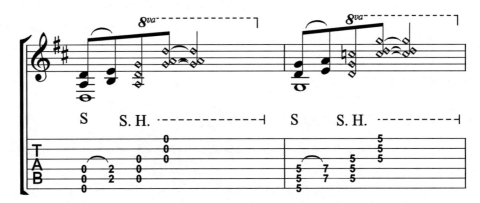

Example 103 shows another percussion effect. This technique is more like a slap bass. Using the flat fingers of your picking hand, slap the bottom two strings sharply on the beat. Your fretting hand plays hammer-ons and pull-offs. No notes are plucked or strummed; the entire segment is played simply by slapping the strings in conjunction with hammer-ons and pull-offs.

EX 103. SLAP BASS LINE

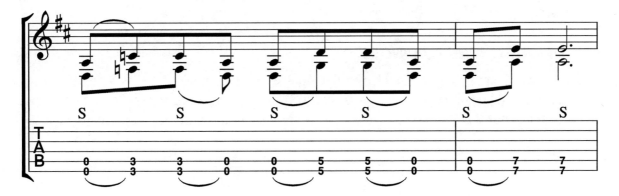

TEN THINGS YOU CAN'T DO IN STANDARD TUNING

If you discuss alternate tunings like DADGAD with other guitarists, sooner or later someone will say "I don't need to use those, I can play anything in standard tuning that you can play in an alternate tuning." While the sentiment is understandable, it's fairly easy to see, and prove, that this statement simply isn't true. Each tuning (including standard) has certain unique characteristics that allow you to play things are difficult, if not impossible, to play in other tunings.

In many cases, the differences between the music that can be created in different tunings can be fairly subtle. You may be able to play the same notes in standard as in DADGAD, but for tunes or arrangements that are meant to be in DADGAD, a standard tuning adaptation is likely to not create quite the same effect. The differences may have to do with the chord voicings that are possible, the interaction of overtones and sympathetic vibrations on the guitar, the location on the neck where the notes are found, differences in fingerings, even the tension of the strings. These may seem like small things, but in the end, we're dealing with the same twelve notes regardless of what tuning we use, and it's the details that make all the difference.

But there are also some differences that are less subjective. Many of these fall into the category of "parlor tricks" that may or may not be musically useful, but some have definite musical applications. So, just for fun, let's look at ten things you can play in DADGAD that you either can't do at all, or at least can't do easily, in standard tuning. Hopefully these will inspire you to create something new, but at least, they can give you some discussion points for the next time someone tells you they can "do it all" in standard tuning!

UNIQUE CHORD VOICINGS

1. FIVE-NOTE FIRST POSITION CHORDS

Surprisingly, a ninth chord consisting of consecutive stacked thirds cannot be played in standard tuning, without altering the voicing. It's easy in DADGAD, however. The shape of an ordinary C chord in standard tuning becomes a C9 in DADGAD, while a slight alteration creates a CMaj9 chord. Try to find a way to play these chord voicings in standard tuning!

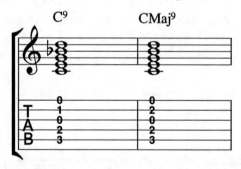

2. TIGHT CHORD VOICINGS

Pianists often use very close, clustered chords, especially in jazz. These chords are difficult to emulate on the guitar, but some are easier in DADGAD. Here is one shape that provides a close cluster of notes. You could play these in standard tuning, if you have really huge hands!

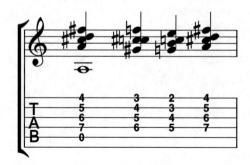

3. ELEVENTH CHORD WITH A THIRD

Guitarists usually eliminate the third of a chord when playing a suspended fourth or eleventh chord. Leaving the third in creates a more dissonant sound that might be desired at times. In standard tuning, guitarists don't usually have a choice, and must choose between the third and fourth. In DADGAD, there are several fingerings that allow both the third and the fourth to be present in a chord.

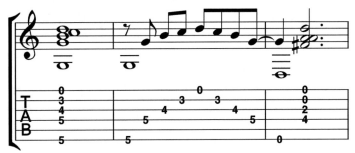

CASCADING HARP EFFECT

4. FOUR SCALE TONES ON FOUR STRINGS

We've already explored the harp-like sound of DADGAD. It is possible to get this sound in any tuning, including standard, but DADGAD makes it very easy. One reason is that sequential scale tones are readily available on adjacent strings. For example, the following simple fingering provides four steps of a scale on four different strings.

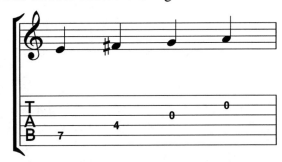

5. FIVE SCALE TONES ON FIVE STRINGS

It's even possible to play five sequential scale steps on five strings in DADGAD. By using the twelfth fret harmonic on the sixth string, we can get five scale steps to sustain at once.

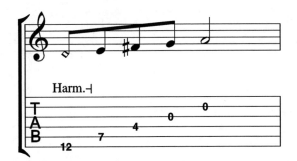

The second interval between the third and fourth strings in DADGAD makes these cross-string sequential scale tones possible.

6. THREE CONSECUTIVE MINOR THIRDS

For an extremely dissonant effect, you can play three notes, each a half-step apart. There are a few ways to get this effect in standard tuning, for some notes, but you can play many different three-note clusters in DADGAD. This one is a bit of a stretch!

7. SIX OF THE SAME NOTE

Is it possible to play the same note on all six strings? It is in DADGAD, although some of the notes will be in different octaves.

This may seem like more of a party trick more than a useful technique, but as shown in the example below, you can get some useful effects from the duplicate notes.

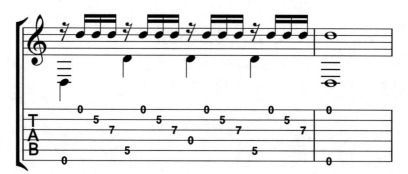

8. ONE FINGER ROCK N' ROLL

Rock guitarists use a shape known as a power chord, which consists of a doubled root and a fifth. In DADGAD, this shape can be played with just one finger.

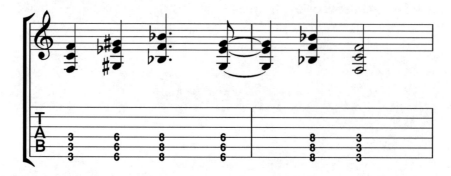

In addition, you can use this basic shape to easily play the classic rock 'n'roll rhythm riff, which requires a bit of a stretch while playing a barre chord in standard tuning.

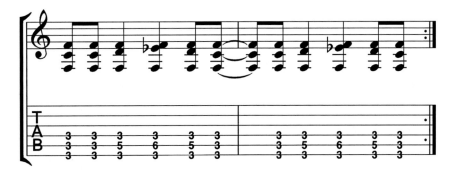

9. UNISONS

We explored unisons in an earlier chapter. Although you can play certain notes in unison in standard tuning, in DADGAD you can play melodic lines or entire scales using unisons.

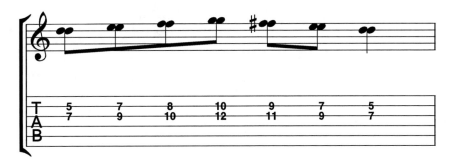

10. HAMMER-ONS IN OCTAVES

Finally, DADGAD is extremely octave-friendly. The example below shows a lick that uses hammer-ons and pull-offs extensively, all in octaves. This lick could be simulated, but certainly not duplicated, in standard tuning.

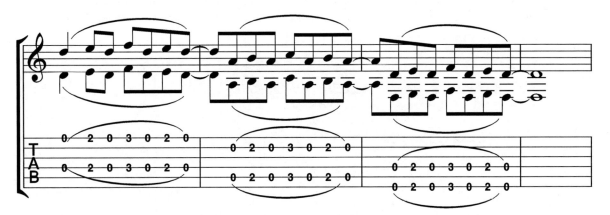

We'll stop at ten examples, but you can surely find more as you explore DADGAD.

PUTTING IT ALL TOGETHER

This chapter has explored various tricks and techniques that are fun to take advantage of in DADGAD. Although most of these techniques are not unique to DADGAD, many of them work particularly well in this tuning. These are just a starting point, however. You'll discover many more as you continue to explore DADGAD.

The tune 'Nuff Said, on the next page, uses many of the techniques we discussed in this chapter. Let's look at the introduction to 'Nuff Said, in Example 104. The tune is built on a repeating bass line, that includes a percussive string hit on beats 2 and 4, simulating a snare drum. Simply bring your thumb down sharply on the strings between the other notes. The introduction adds a harmonic that alternates between the fifth, seventh, and twelfth frets. Try to keep the harmonic ringing as you play the bass line.

TRACK 54

EX 104. RHYTHM GROOVE FROM 'NUFF SAID

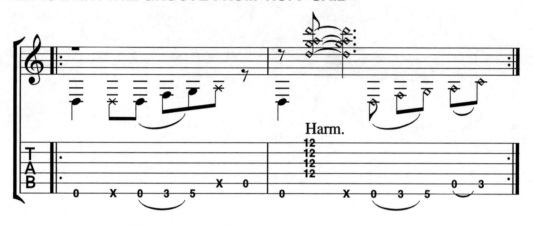

This bassline is the basis of the tune. When the melody starts at measure 11 it uses parallel harmony over a simplified version of this bass line. Each two-bar phrase is answered by the introductory bass line, providing the illusion that the bass line continues throughout the tune.

Example 105 shows the first few bars from the B section of this tune. This phrase combines open strings with some cross string picking patterns. Notice that the notes played by the thumb cross over to the higher strings and become part of the melody.

TRACK 55

EX 105. CROSS STRING PATTERN FROM 'NUFF SAID

As you try 'Nuff Said, watch for harmonics, octaves, unisons, cross string techniques, parallel harmony, hammer-ons, pull-offs, and other techniques discussed in this chapter.

EX. 106. 'NUFF SAID

'Nuff Said

Doug Young

80

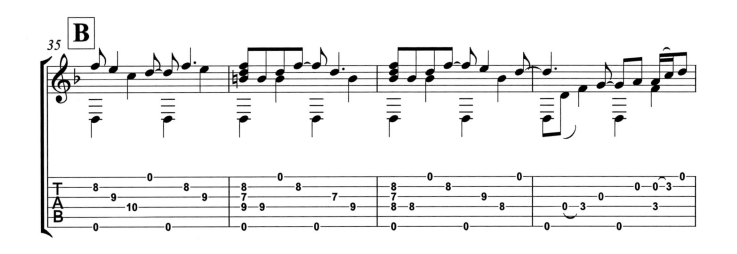

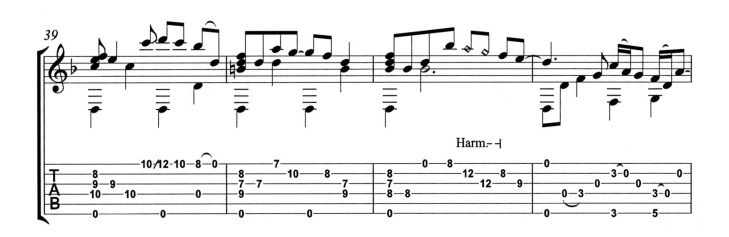

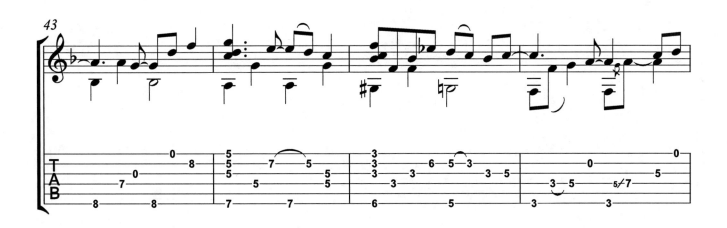

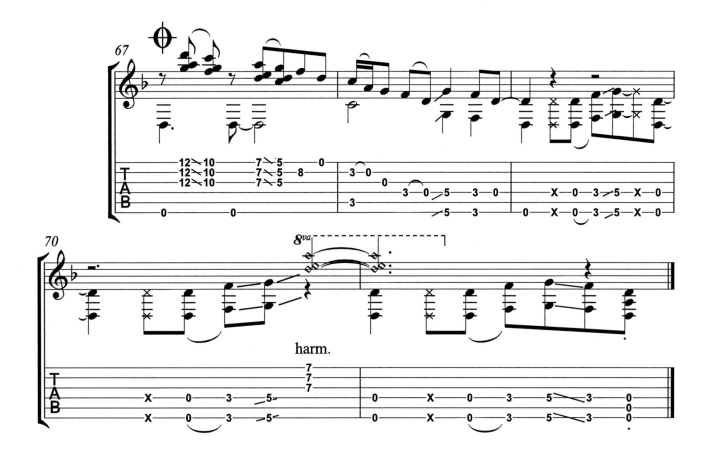

CHORD PROGRESSIONS

When playing in alternate tunings, guitarists often ignore chord progressions to explore the sound of droning open strings. It's a good sound, but knowing some common chord progressions in DADGAD allows you to break out of that sound when you want to, and allows you to play a broader range of music.

Although there are an almost unlimited number of possible chord progressions, everyone should know a few basic patterns. Blues progressions are very common in many different styles, and variations on the I-IV-V chord sequences are extremely common in folk and rock tunes. In jazz and pop standards, the ii-V-I progression occurs frequently. A progression known as "Rhythm Changes" is also common in jazz. Learning these basic progressions in DADGAD will get you started exploring different sounds in DADGAD and allow you to stay in DADGAD in cases where you might be tempted to return to standard tuning.

WHAT YOU'LL LEARN IN THIS CHAPTER

MOVEABLE FORM CHORD PROGRESSIONS

Learning chord progressions based on movable forms is very efficient because once you've learned the chords and the progression in one key, you can play in as many as twelve different keys, just by shifting positions. We'll look at some easy shapes and sequences of shapes that make this possible in DADGAD.

OPEN STRING CHORD PROGRESSIONS

Playing standard chord progressions doesn't mean you have to leave behind the sound that attracted you to DADGAD in the first place. We can incorporate open strings, cross string patterns, and unusual chords into standard chord progressions as well.

THE BLUES PROGRESSION

One of the most common chord progressions is the twelve bar blues, which uses the I, IV and V chords of a key in a standard sequence. We've already seen many examples that use these three chords in various keys, but let's look specifically at the blues progression. There are many variations of the twelve bar blues progression, but the basic pattern is simply:

$$I / IV / I / I / IV / IV / I / I / V / IV / I / V$$

The V chord is typically a seventh chord, and often all three chords are sevenths. Example 107 shows one set of chords you can use to play a blues progression in DADGAD. The example is in A, so the chords are A7, D7, and E7.

EX 107. TWELVE BAR BLUES IN A. WITH MOVEABLE CHORDS

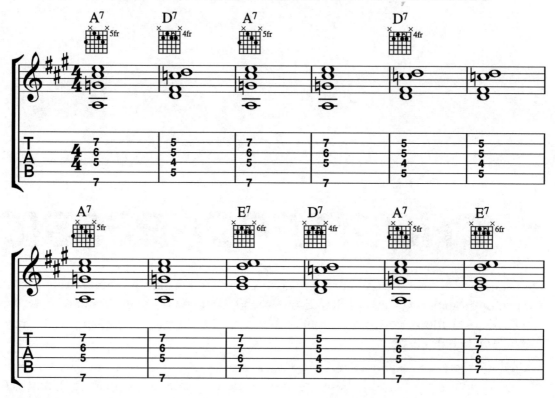

Because these are moveable shapes, you can use them to play in almost any key. For example, sliding up three frets lets you play the same progression in C. Example 108 shows the same blues pattern in C.

EX 108. TWELVE BAR BLUES PROGRESSION IN THE KEY OF C

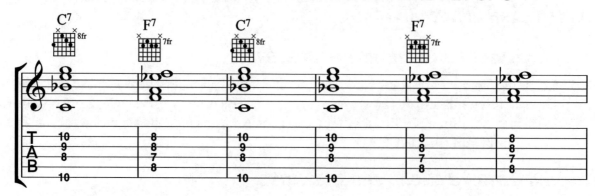

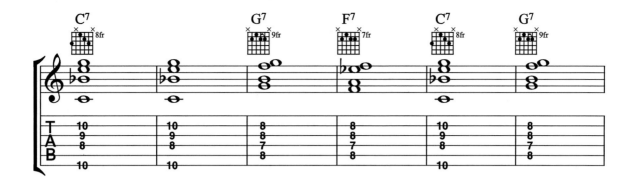

Example 109 provides a more complex example using moveable chord shapes. The example adds a constant quarter note bass, known as a monotonic bass, and enhances the chord progression by moving up and down by half steps in various places. This is just a mechanism to add some tension and interest to the chord progression.

TRACK 57

EX 109. TWELVE BAR BLUES IN A OVER A MONOTONIC BASS

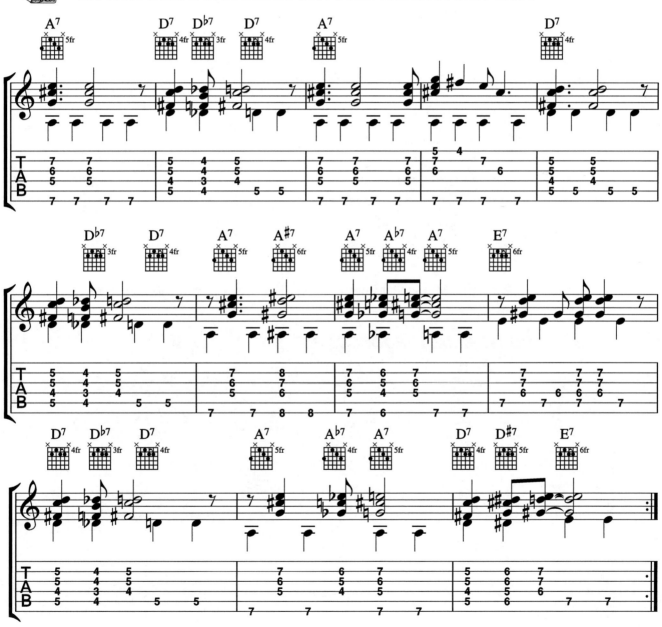

BLUES PROGRESSION WITH MINIMALIST CHORDS

There is a trick you may know from standard tuning that involves using a simple two-note chord shape as seventh chords. The same idea can also be used in DADGAD. Example 110 shows how a single shape can function as an A7, D7, and E7, simply by sliding up or down one fret. The shape uses the third and seventh of each chord, which are the most important notes in defining the quality of the chord. The bass is implied.

EX 110. MINIMALIST SEVENTH CHORDS

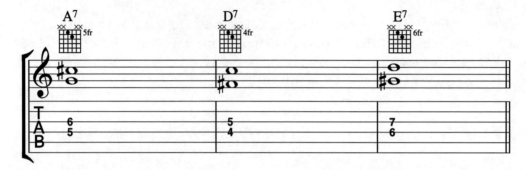

These shapes also work at the eleventh fret in A major, and you can also move them to any key.

EX 111. MINIMALIST SEVENTH CHORDS

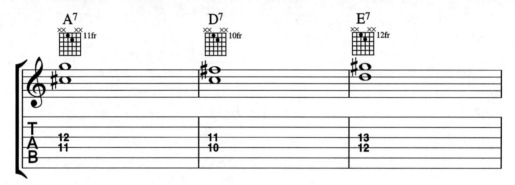

Example 112 demonstrates a blues progression using these partial chords. Notice how you can hear the chord changes, even without a bass line.

EXAMPLE 112. BLUES PROGRESSION

One reason these shapes are useful is that they free your fingers to add additional notes. You might add more notes to the chords to make them more interesting, or you can play melodies along with the chords. Example 113 provides one example. Because the example is in A, the open A and D strings are available as bass notes. The chords are interspersed between the melody line.

TRACK 58

EX 113. TWELVE BAR BLUES IN A, WITH MINIMALIST CHORDS

THE II-V-I PROGRESSION

One of the most common chord sequences in jazz as well as many popular standards is the ii-V-I progression. The ii chord is the minor chord built on the second step of the scale in a given key, while the V chord is a dominant seventh chord built on the fifth step of the scale. For example, in the key of C, the ii-V-I progression would be Dm, G7, C. These chords can also be modified and extended while keeping the basic function the same. For example, a tune might use Dm9, G13, Cmaj7, or Dm7, G7$\sharp$5, CMaj9.

Let's start with some examples using open string chords. These chords tend to exploit the unique sounds DADGAD offers and can add interesting twists to the usual ii-V-I sound. Example 114 shows a ii-V-I sequence in C, using two sets of chords.

TRACK 59

EX 114. II-V-I PROGRESSION IN C MAJOR

Example 115 uses chord shapes based on the tenths patterns we explored earlier to play a ii-V-I in G major. These shapes work for many different keys.

TRACK 60

EX 115. II-V-I PROGRESSION IN G MAJOR

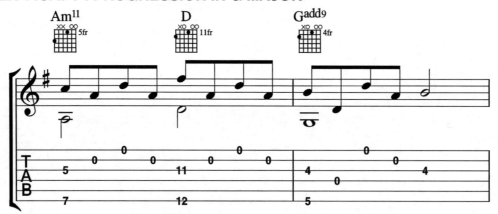

Understanding chord progressions and knowing where to find them in different keys can be helpful when creating an accompaniment, but they can also be useful for solo arrangements, composing, or just noodling on the guitar. Example 116 creates a melodic line that uses some of the scale techniques we explored earlier, based on a ii-V-I chord progression. The chord diagrams indicate how you might visualize the chords, even when you don't need to finger the full shapes.

EX 116. II-V-I PROGRESSION IN G MAJOR

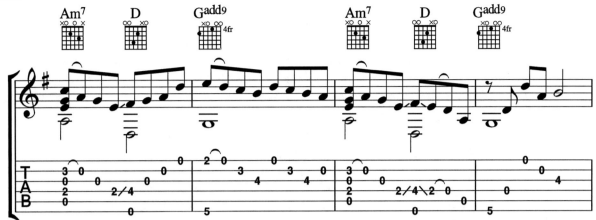

A good way to get comfortable with playing ii-V-I progressions in any key is to play a cycle of chord changes that runs through many different keys. Any pattern of chord changes and keys will do, as long as the pattern forces you to move through keys you wouldn't otherwise explore. If you run into a chord that you don't know, stop and figure it out.

Example 117 demonstrates one such exercise. This example starts with an Am. An Am is the ii chord in the key of G, so the second chord will be a D7, the V chord in G, followed by G major. From there, the example moves to G minor. G minor is the ii chord in the key of F, so we will follow the Gm with a C7 and then an F. Next, the pattern moves to F minor, and so on. Notice that this pattern leads to the key of D♭. There are no open string chords for the key of D♭ in DADGAD, but there are other fingerings that work.

EX 117. PRACTICING CYCLING THROUGH II-V-I CHORDS

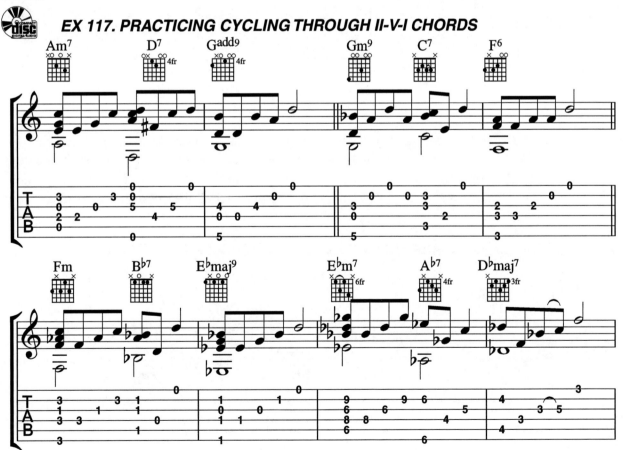

MOVEABLE II-V-I CHORD PATTERNS

Very simple tunes may stay in one key, but many tunes modulate to different keys. This is especially true when playing jazz tunes or standards based on ii-V-I progressions. These songs often move through many different keys, often changing keys very quickly.

To be able to play any chord progression in any key, it's easiest to use moveable chord shapes. Below are a few moveable chord shapes you can use for a ii-V-I chord progression. These are in the key of F, but since these shapes are movable, you can use them for almost any key.

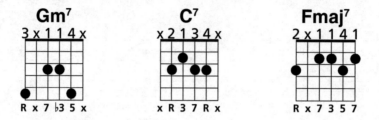

Example 118 applies these shapes, moving through several keys.

EX 118. CHORD PROGRESSION WITH MOVEABLE II-V-I SHAPES

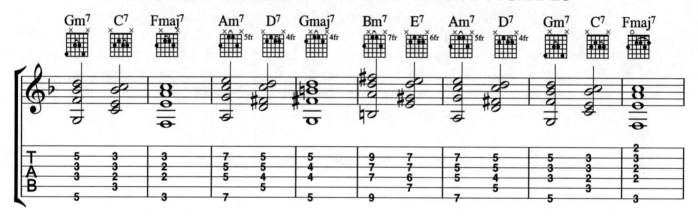

WALKING BASS

These moveable chord shapes work well for jazzy walking bass patterns. Try Example 119 with a swing feel, paying close attention to the fingering of the bass notes. The chords should be played with a jazz "comping" feel, short and staccato (listen to the recording). It's more important to play the bass line with a solid rhythm and feel than to get all the notes in the chords.

TRACK 63

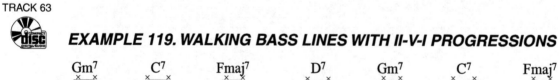

EXAMPLE 119. WALKING BASS LINES WITH II-V-I PROGRESSIONS

92

ALTERED CHORDS

If you play jazz or popular standards, you have probably encountered more complex chords known as altered chords, in which certain notes are raised or lowered. There are many different alterations found in jazz. Minor chords often have a lowered fifth. Dominant seventh chords typically have raised or lowered fifths and ninths. Major chords are often extended to become major seventh, major ninth, or even major thirteenth chords.

Below is one set of altered chords you can use in a typical ii-V-I progression.

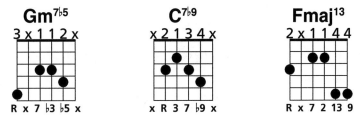

There are many possible variations of these chords, especially dominant seventh chords. Here are a few possibilities.

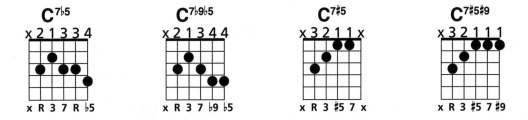

These chords are all moveable, so you can transpose them to any key you need. Example 120 offers a brief look at how you might use these types of chords.

TRACK 64

EX 120. CHORD PROGRESSION WITH ALTERED II-V-I CHORDS

RHYTHM CHANGES

Most jazz players are familiar with a chord progression known as "Rhythm Changes." The chords originally came from the tune "I've Got Rhythm," but were adopted and modified for many jazz standards and eventually became a standard progression, somewhat like the blues chord progression. It's a good chord sequence to know, and it also serves as an exercise in figuring out how to play something in DADGAD that you might not normally play. Working on a chord progression like this, or selecting a tune from a song book and working out the chords in DAGDAD is a great way to see if you really know your chords, or to motivate you to work out new ones.

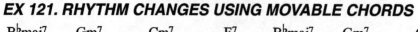

EX 121. RHYTHM CHANGES USING MOVABLE CHORDS

RHYTHM CHANGES USING OPEN STRING CHORDS

Now let's see if we can make this chord progression more "DADGAD-like", and incorporate some chords that use open strings and some more interesting colors. Example 122 demonstrates the rhythm changes progression in B♭, using open string chords and a fingerpicking pattern.

TRACK 65

EX 122. RHYTHM CHANGES WITH OPEN STRING CHORDS

SCALES AND ARPEGGIOS

Like the letters of the alphabet, scales are fundamental building blocks from which many other musical elements are derived. Scales are essential tools for rock and jazz players and are a great way to improve technique and to develop improvisational skills. But even for fingerstyle players, it's useful to have a command of scales, and learning scales in DADGAD can help you feel more at home in the tuning.

Arpeggios are broken chords - basically, the notes of a chord played sequentially. Like scales, knowing some patterns for arpeggios can help you know your way around the fretboard. Arppegios are also especially useful when picking out melodies.

There are two types of scales and arpeggios that are useful in DADGAD: moveable and cross-string. We'll explore each of these in this chapter.

WHAT YOU'LL LEARN IN THIS CHAPTER

MOVEABLE SCALES

On the guitar, moveable scales form geometric patterns that can be played anywhere on the fretboard. If you know a C moveable scale, you can move the same fingering up one fret to play a C♯ scale, for example. We'll discover enough moveable scale patterns to be able to play major and minor scales almost anywhere on the fretboard, in any key.

CROSS-STRING SCALES

Cross-string scales take advantage of both the open strings and the interval relationships in DADGAD to create a harp-like effect. We've seen examples of this technique already, but in this chapter, we'll look systematically at cross-string scale patterns in several keys.

ARPEGGIOS

We'll look at some common arpeggio patterns for major, minor and seventh chords in DADGAD.

MOVABLE MAJOR SCALES

There are five basic scale shapes that can be used to play major scales, each of which correspond to a chord shape in the CAGED system. You may want to review the discussion of the CAGED system earlier in this book before moving on. Example 123 shows a C major scale in the first position. We'll refer to this scale pattern as the "C" form, because you can visualize the notes of the scale as coming from the C shape in the CAGED system.

EX 123. C MAJOR SCALE. "C" FORM

The relationship between this scale pattern and the C chord shape is easiest to see with a fretboard diagram. For example, the C chord shape in DADGAD is on the left, below. On the right is a diagram of the fretboard, with the notes of the associated scale shown as boxes and circles. The boxed notes are the notes that form the C chord shape. Although the scale in Example 123 uses open strings, remember that both the chord and the scale are really moveable shapes. You can find this chord shape, and the associated scale, anywhere on the fretboard.

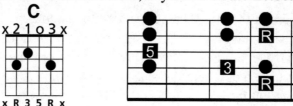

To see the pattern without open strings more clearly, let's move the shape up the fretboard to a D, as shown in Example 124.

EX 124. D MAJOR SCALE. "C" FORM

Of course, you can move this pattern to any location on the neck, to play in any key. First, make sure you understand how this scale relates to the "C" chord shape. Then locate different chords up and down the fretboard using this shape, and play the scale form at that location.

Next, let's look at the scale that corresponds to the "A" shape. Example 125 shows a C Major scale based on the A chord shape.

EX 125. C MAJOR SCALE. "A" FORM

The following fretboard diagram and chord shape shows the relationship graphically. It's easiest to think of the simple "power chord" form of the A shape when locating this scale. The root note on the fourth string can be played in one of two places: on the fourth string, as indicated by the square box in the diagram, or as the note two frets lower on the second string. The note on the third string matches the chord form being used for visualization, but when playing the scale, the note on the second string falls more naturally under the fingers. When playing melodies made from the notes of this scale pattern, you may find occasion to use either or both of these options.

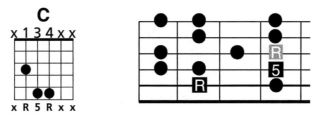

The next scale pattern corresponds to the "G" chord form in the CAGED system. The lowest root note is outside of the position. Remember that the goal is to know where all the notes of a scale are located, not necessarily to be able to play a scale up and down from root to root.

EX 126. C MAJOR SCALE. "G" FORM

Here is the "G" shape for a C chord, and the associated fretboard diagram. The gray square is the root, C, which is a bit out of position.

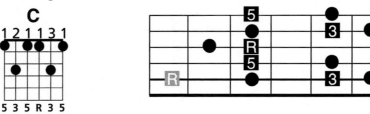

Example 127 shows the "E" form. The C major scale using this form is located at the seventh position. The second note of the scale requires you to move out of position, but the rest of the scale lays very comfortably between the seventh and tenth frets.

EX 127. C MAJOR SCALE, "E" FORM

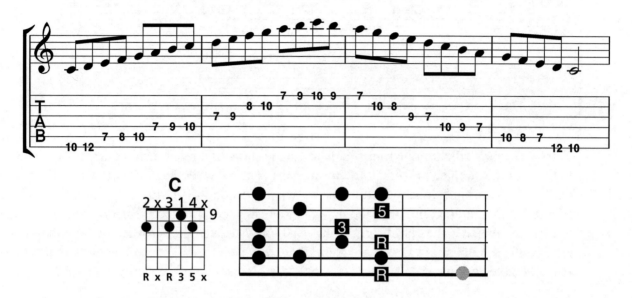

For C major, the "D" form can be found in the tenth position, between the tenth and fourteenth frets. If this is too high to play on your guitar, learn the pattern using another key by moving down a few frets.

EX 128. C MAJOR SCALE, "D" FORM

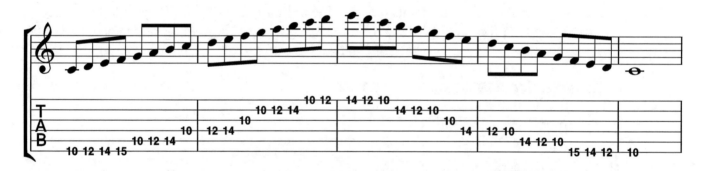

Here are the chord and fretboard diagrams for the D scale form. This scale should look familiar; we looked at this pattern using open strings in the first chapter of this book. Notice that, other than the fourth note of the scale on the sixth string, the entire pattern uses the same frets across all six strings. The notes in gray on the third string are duplicated on the second string, and are optional.

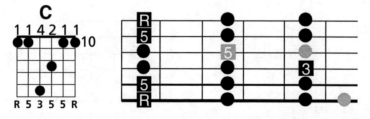

LEARNING SCALE FORMS

To be able to play melodies using these scales, you need to be able to play them anywhere on the fretboard, in any key. There are several ways to practice and memorize these scales. Example 129 shows one useful exercise, using the "E" scale form. Play a chord, followed by the scale form for that chord. Then, move up the neck and play a chord a step higher, and play that scale form. Say the name of each chord as you play, and focus on the shape of the chord and scale.

EX 129. PLAYING A SCALE PATTERN UP THE NECK

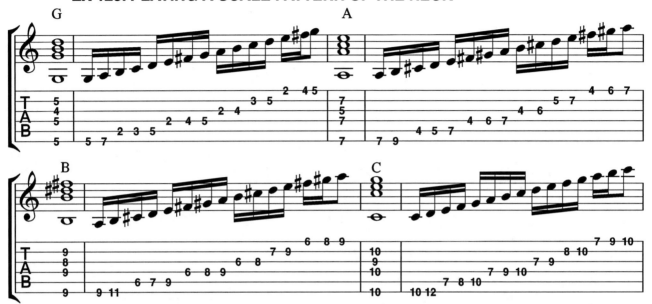

Next, pick one of the CAGED form chords somewhere on the neck, and play the associated scale pattern. Then find a chord near the same position whose root is a five notes higher, and play the scale associated with the form. Continue until you have played all five shapes.

EX 130. PLAYING ALL SCALE PATTERNS IN ONE POSITION

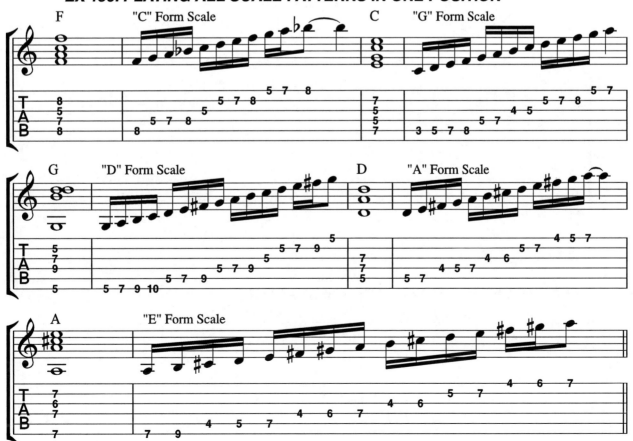

SCALE PATTERNS

Besides picking out melodies, a good way to really learn the notes of a scale, as well as improve your technique, is to practice various scale patterns. Let's look at a few examples. Ideally, you want to practice these patterns over all five scale forms, in as many keys as possible, until these scale shapes become comfortable and fall under your fingers automatically.

Example 131 is a pattern of four notes, sequenced up the scale one step at a time. The pattern is based on the "A" form of a C major scale.

EX 131. ASCENDING FOUR-NOTE PATTERN

Example 132 is the reverse of Example 131, with the pattern played descending the scale.

EX 132. DESCENDING FOUR-NOTE PATTERN

Example 133 combines the ascending and descending pattern, still based on the "A" form scale.

EX 133. ASCENDING AND DESCENDING FOUR-NOTE PATTERNS

Example 134 shows an "every-other note" pattern.

EX 134. EVERY OTHER NOTE SCALE PATTERN

Example 135 is a three note sequence, played in triplets.

EX 135. THREE-NOTE SCALE PATTERN

Example 136 reverses the direction of each set of three notes.

EX 136. ASCENDING AND DESCENDING THREE-NOTE PATTERN

Example 137 is a short melody that uses some of these patterns in a more musical context. Notice that this example uses hammer-ons and pull-offs extensively, which produces more musical phrasing. It's a good idea to practice all the patterns described here with hammer-ons and pull-offs wherever possible.

TRACK 66

EX 137. USING SCALE PATTERNS IN A MELODY

103

MINOR SCALES

Minor scales are more interesting than major scales, because there are many more variations and harmonic opportunities with minor scales. Before looking at the moveable minor scale forms, let's look at the four most common forms of minor scales, using simple first position D minor scales.

The D *natural minor* scale shares the same notes as the key of F major, since D minor is the relative minor of F. Example 138 shows one way to play a D natural minor scale.

EX 138. D NATURAL MINOR

Another minor scale that is common, especially in modal music, is the *dorian* scale. D dorian shares the notes of the C major scale. You can build any dorian scale by starting on the second note of a major scale, and playing to the octave above. If you compare the D dorian scale in Example 139 with the natural minor scale in Example 138, you will notice that the only difference is the sixth step of the scale, which is a B natural in the D dorian scale and a B♭ in the D natural minor scale.

EX 139. D DORIAN MINOR

The *harmonic minor* scale was designed to create a stronger resolution when moving from the V chord (an A7 in the key of D) to the root, and therefore D harmonic minor has a C♯ as the seventh step of the scale. The other notes of the D harmonic scale are the same as a D natural minor.

EX 140. D HARMONIC MINOR

The harmonic minor scale contains a big jump between the sixth and seventh steps of the scale, which sounds exotic, but also is a bit awkward. The *melodic minor* scale "fixes" this issue by raising the sixth step of the scale to a B natural. The result, as seen in Example 141, is a scale you could think of as a combination of the dorian scale and the harmonic minor scale.

EX 141. D MELODIC MINOR

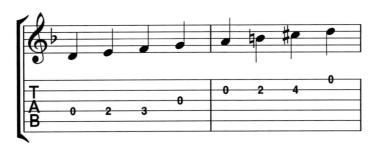

One of the reasons minor keys offer more possibilities than major keys is because of the many variations of minor scales from which you can choose. When playing in a minor key, it's not necessary to limit ourselves to just one of these scales. You may be able to use more than one, or even all of them. If we combine the possible variations of the minor scales, we can create a composite D minor scale that has both the lowered and raised sixth, as well as the lowered and raised seventh, as seen in Example 142.

EX 142. A COMPOSITE D MINOR SCALE

Composers often take advantage of these different notes in minor scales and emphasize the altered notes for effect. These extra notes, often played as a descending bass line, are the basis of many well known songs, from jazz standards like *My Funny Valentine* to the rock classic *Stairway to Heaven*. Example 143 shows how we can leverage all four scale variations in a fingerstyle arrangement. Notice the presence of all four of the notes that characterize the different forms of the D minor scale, first in the bass line, then in the upper voice.

TRACK 67

EX 143. EXAMPLE BASED ON A COMPOSITE D MINOR SCALE

MOVABLE MINOR SCALES

The movable minor scales are slightly more awkward to play, and require a bit of stretching compared to the major scales. We'll look at just two forms of each type of minor scale to get you started. Example 144 shows the minor scales associated with the A minor shape, but in the key of C minor. (Recall that the CAGED system can be applied to minor chord shapes as well.) The chord around which the scales can be visualized is played at the beginning of the example.

EX 144. C MINOR SCALES, "A MINOR FORM"

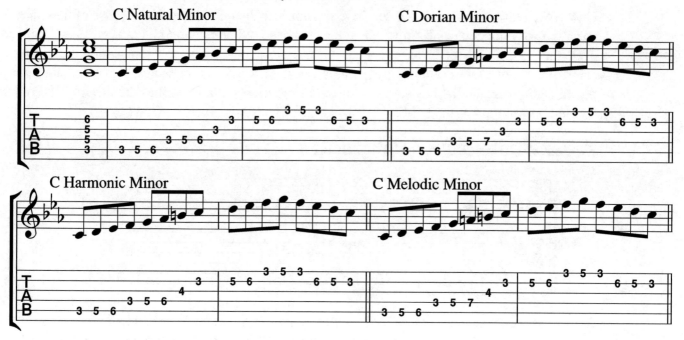

Example 145 shows the C minor scales that correspond to the D minor chord shape.

EX 145. C MINOR SCALES, "D MINOR FORM"

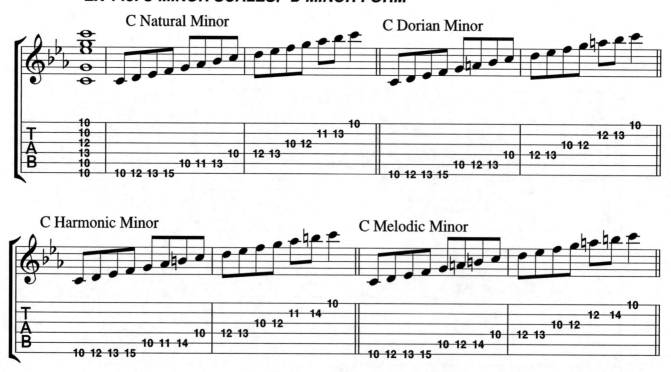

MINOR SCALE PATTERNS

As with major scales, you can move these minor scale patterns around the fretboard, and can also play them in nearly endless patterns. Example 146 shows a four note scale pattern in A minor.

EX 146. FOUR-NOTE SCALE PATTERN IN A MINOR

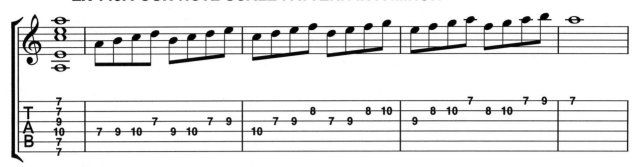

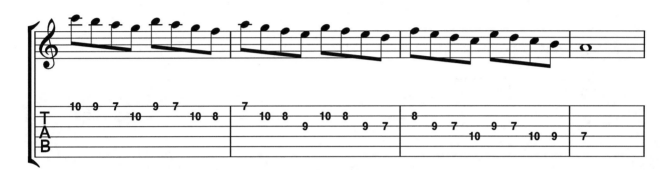

Practicing these scale patterns can be very helpful when playing melodies. Example 147 provides one example, using a melody in A minor, based on the same scale form shown in Examples 145 and 146. This example adds bass notes, as well as hammer-ons and pull-offs to create a more musical exercise.

TRACK 68

EX 147. USING SCALE PATTERNS IN A MELODY

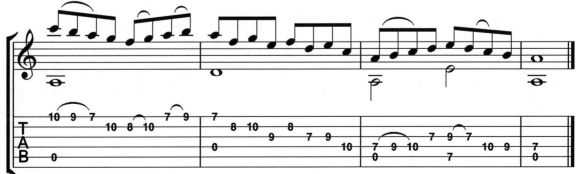

CROSS-STRING SCALES

We've looked at cross-string patterns earlier in this book, so you've discovered the appeal of their harp-like sound. Cross-string scales are more difficult to learn because the patterns are not moveable, so you need to memorize different patterns for every key. Fingerings are also critical with most cross-string patterns, but the sound is so compelling that the extra effort is worthwhile.

It is possible to play almost any scale using a combination of open strings and cross-string notes, and the possible arrangements of notes and fingerings for these scales is almost endless. The fingerings shown here are just one way to play these scales, and you may want to try to discover more on your own. The basic principle is to find the next note at any point of the scale on a different string than the one you're currently playing. This isn't always possible, but as long as you can keep some notes ringing, you will create the intended effect

Example 148 shows a C major scale, starting with the lowest C note. The stretches from the seventh to the third fret will take some effort, but try to hold down both notes at once!

Note: Examples 148 through 156 are all on the same CD track.

TRACK 69

EX 148. CROSS-STRING C MAJOR SCALE

Example 149 is an alternate way to play a cross-string C major scale, combining hammer-ons, pull-offs, and slides with the open strings. Try to play this as smoothly as you can to blend with the sound of the open strings.

TRACK 69

EX 149. CROSS-STRING C MAJOR SCALE

Examples 150 through 153 are cross string scales in various keys. There are many possible fingerings for these scales, but these patterns should give you some idea of the options. Some of these stretches may seem impossible, and in some cases, you will not be able to hold adjacent strings down as long as you might like. Just focus on sustaining each note as long as you can and play a smoothly as you can.

EX 150. CROSS-STRING D MAJOR SCALE

EX 151. CROSS-STRING F MAJOR SCALE

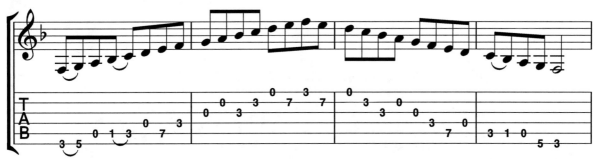

EX 152. CROSS-STRING G MAJOR SCALE

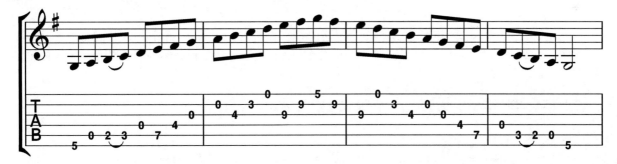

EX 153. CROSS-STRING A MAJOR SCALE

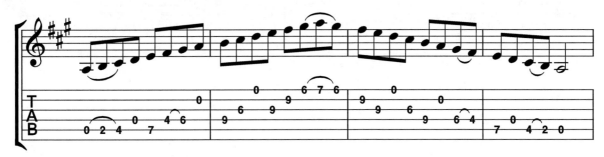

MINOR CROSS-STRING SCALES

Of course, you can play minor scales using cross-string techniques as well. Here are a few examples. Example 154 is a two-octave D minor scale.

TRACK 69

EX 154. CROSS-STRING D MINOR SCALE

Example 155 is a two octave G minor scale.

TRACK 69

EX 155. CROSS-STRING G MINOR SCALE

Example 156 uses a hammer-on to avoid an unreasonable stretch. In the second measure, sliding on the second string from the third fret to the seventh fret may make the position change easier.

TRACK 69

EX 156. CROSS-STRING A MINOR SCALE

As we've already seen, there are many forms of minor scales. All of them can be played using cross-string fingerings, although you may have to make some substantial adjustments in fingering to accommodate the different forms.

Example 157 shows cross-string versions of four forms of a C minor scale.

EX 157. CROSS-STRING C MINOR SCALES

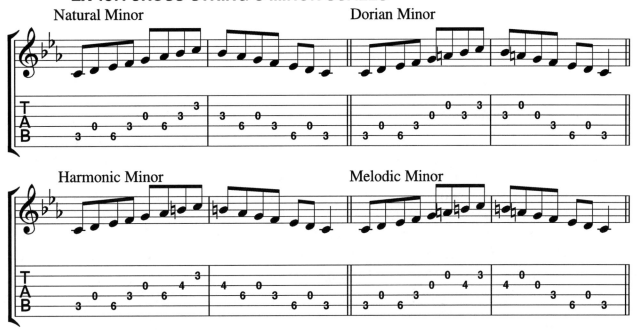

In some cases, it is difficult to maintain a strict cross-string approach. Example 158 shows four forms of an E minor scale. The melodic and harmonic minor forms use slides in a few places to produce reasonable fingering.

EX 158. CROSS-STRING E MINOR SCALES

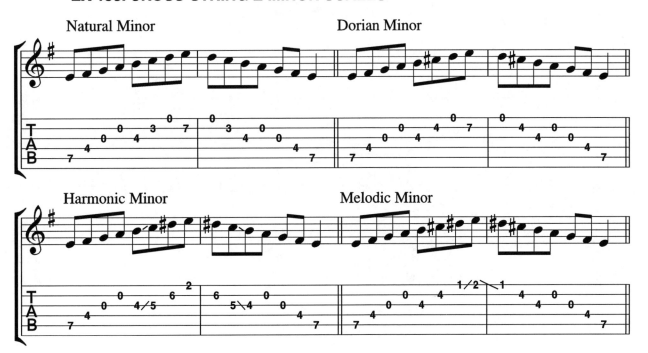

111

CROSS-STRING EXAMPLES

Example 159 uses a cross-string scale in a melodic example. This exercise consists of exactly the same notes as Example 147, which demonstrates the application of various scale patterns. Example 159 applies these same patterns in a cross-string approach. These two examples also show how you can refinger a melody to achieve a cross-string effect. You may want to revisit Example 147 before trying the cross-string version and compare the two versions.

To create the intended effect in Example 159, pay close attention to the fingerings, and try to keep as many notes sounding at once as possible. Except for a few spots, it should be possible to have at least two, and often three or four melody strings ringing at once. To accomplish this, you have to be careful to not lift your fingers any sooner than necessary. It's also important to avoid accidently damping any strings.

For example, look at the first measure. After playing the first note on the open second string, play the third string, fourth fret, leaving the second string ringing. Delay fingering the third note until the last possible moment, to keep the second string ringing. Hold down the notes on the second and third strings while you play the fourth note on the open first string. Continue to hold the second and third strings down through the rest of the measure. In the second measure, try to keep the second and third strings held down throughout the measure. Holding down strings even longer than may seem necessary will help enhance the harp effect.

Some of the suggested fingerings in Example 159 are a bit of a stretch, so take your time. There are many different fingerings, and some notes could be played in other locations with similar results, so don't be afraid to experiment with alternatives once you are comfortable with the example as written, or if you find the stretches too difficult.

TRACK 70

EX 159. CROSS-STRING MELODIC EXAMPLE

Example 160 is a longer example, in D minor. The suggested fingerings in the first two measures allow the notes to ring as long as possible. In measure 3, try to partially lift the barre, continuing to hold the bass and last melody note while you play the open strings on the third beat.

TRACK 71

EX 160. CROSS-STRING MELODIC EXAMPLE IN D MINOR

113

ARPEGGIOS

Arpeggios are broken chords, and consist of the notes of a chord, played one note at a time. One form of arpeggio is almost automatic for guitarists. If you fingerpick a chord pattern, an arpeggio naturally results. In this case, the notes in the arpeggio are determined by the chord fingering, and the notes may be in various orders, across the strings. When playing melodies, it is also useful to be able to play arpeggios in their musical order. For example, an arpeggio of a C major triad would consist of the notes C, E, G, in order. If you extend the arpeggio into multiple octaves, it would repeat, C, E, G, C, E, G and so on. Example 161 shows a simple C major arpeggio.

EX 161. C MAJOR ARPEGGIO

You can create arpeggios that correspond to every flavor of chord. For example, Example 162 shows a C minor arpeggio:

EX 162. C MINOR ARPEGGIO

Example 163 is a dominant seventh C arpeggio. Because a seventh chord has four notes, this arpeggio pattern is longer, with each octave outlining the four notes of the chord.

EX 163. C SEVENTH ARPEGGIO

The major seventh arpeggio creates a pretty-sounding pattern. Notice that these extended arpeggios are easier to finger than arpeggios based on triads.

EX 164. C MAJOR SEVENTH ARPEGGIO

The C arpeggios on the previous page are all moveable shapes, so you can slide them up the neck to create an arpeggio in any key you like. You should be able to find arpeggios that correspond to each of the CAGED chord shapes.

Let's look at another set of examples, in the key of G:

EX 165. G MAJOR ARPEGGIO

EX 166. G MINOR ARPEGGIO

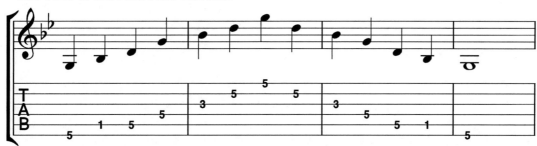

EX 167. G SEVENTH ARPEGGIO

EX 168. G MAJOR SEVENTH ARPEGGIO

EX 169. G MINOR SEVENTH ARPEGGIO

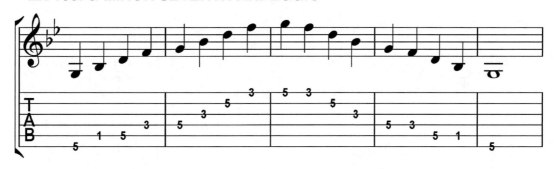

CROSS-STRING ARPEGGIOS

Arpeggios also work very well with the cross string techniques we've applied to scales. Example 170 is a D major seventh arpeggio in which most notes are played on adjacent strings.

EX 170. CROSS-STRING D MAJOR SEVENTH ARPEGGIO

Although Example 170 is not movable because it uses open strings, you can use similar approaches for many different arpeggios. Example 171 is a G major seventh arpeggio that again uses open strings and cross string techniques to create a harp-like effect.

EX 171. CROSS-STRING G MAJOR SEVENTH ARPEGGIO

Arpeggios that include higher chord elements - sevenths, ninths, thirteenths, and so on - offer many more opportunities for cross-string techniques, and begin to sound similar to the cross string scales we looked at earlier. Example 172 is an extended, two octave D Major scale that includes the major seventh and the sixth (or thirteenth). You could consider this to be a D major thirteenth arpeggio, or a D major seventh with an added sixth.

EX 172. D MAJOR THIRTEENTH ARPEGGIO

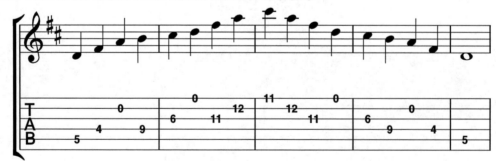

Example 173 is a similar arpeggio in C, with both a major seventh and a sixth.

EX 173. C MAJOR THIRTEENTH ARPEGGIO

116

EXPLORING DIFFERENT KEYS

By now, you should have a good knowledge of DADGAD, and have seen enough chord shapes and scales to be able to play in almost any key. In this chapter, we'll explore some of the more interesting keys that work well in DADGAD. For each key, we'll look at a few representative chords in the key and look at some examples of common chord progressions. Finally, we will look at a musical example in each key.

WHAT YOU'LL LEARN IN THIS CHAPTER

COMMON CHORDS IN VARIOUS KEYS

We'll see a few typical chords for each of the most common chords in each key we explore.

CHORD PROGRESSIONS IN EACH KEY

A good way to explore any new key is to work out some common chord progressions in the key. We'll see how to play I-IV-V and ii-V-I chord sequences in each key.

AN EXAMPLE TUNE IN VARIOUS KEYS

Each key has certain benefits that can be exploited in DADGAD. Although the possibilities are limited only by our imaginations, we'll see a representative example of a tune in each key.

C MAJOR

The key of C is a very comfortable key in DADGAD. The first position C chord is easy to play and the open A and D strings provide C6, Cadd9, or C6/9 sounds, which are very open and rich. All common chords in the key have simple easy fingerings in the first position. All three notes of the open strings are scale tones in C, which supports many open chords and cross-string melody lines.

COMMON CHORDS

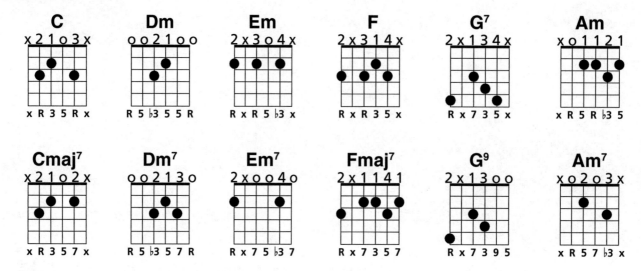

TRACK 72

EX 174. I-IV-V CHORD PROGRESSION IN C

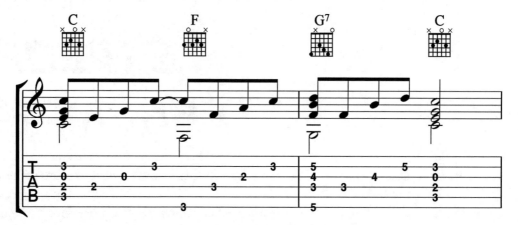

TRACK 73

EX 175. I-VI-II-V-I CHORD PROGRESSION IN C

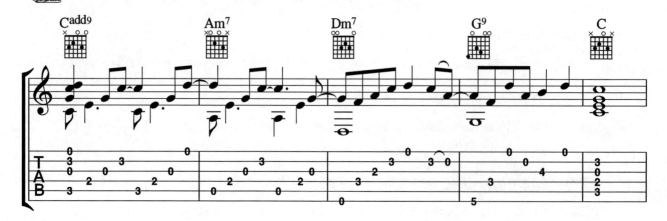

Example 176 is a short tune in the key of C. The tune is built on a I-vi-IV-V chord progression and uses arpeggios based on the chord shapes for most of the melody. Let the notes ring, especially the notes that are tied between measures. These notes usually anticipate the next chord change. Measures 9-12 provide a short bridge section that moves to A minor.

TRACK 74

EX 176. AN EXAMPLE TUNE IN C

119

D MAJOR

The key of D is, of course, the most obvious key to use with DADGAD, and the low Ds on the sixth and fourth strings provide a solid foundation for any tune in D. The third string provides a suspended sound which, combined with the lack of a third on open strings, creates a distinctive open modal sound. We've naturally explored the key of D extensively already in this book.

COMMON CHORDS

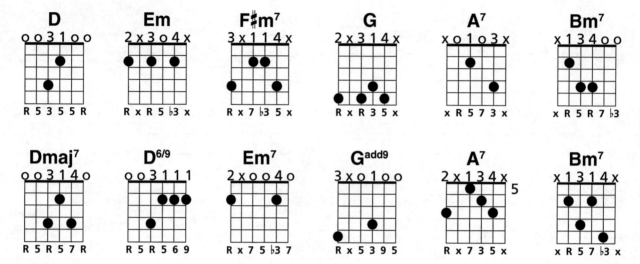

TRACK 75

EX 177. I-IV-V CHORD PROGRESSION

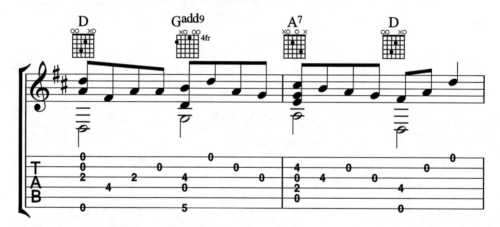

TRACK 76

EX 178. II-V-I PROGRESSION IN D

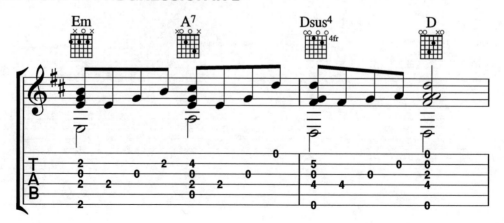

Example 179 demonstrates many of the chords and techniques explored in this book in the key of D. The main theme, starting at measure one, is based on the first position D major scale we encountered in the first chapter of this book. Here, the melody incorporates a variety of hammer-ons, pull-offs, and slides, as well as some fast chord movements.

Measure eight, in the first ending, uses a new technique. The cascading run is played with pull-offs. The challenge is to play the C♯ (fourth fret of the second string) and hold it while playing the B on the fourth fret of the third string. Then, pull-off the C♯ to the open A string, followed by a pull-off on the third string. Finally, the last note of the measure is played as a hammer-on from nowhere. You could pick these notes instead, but the hammer-on and pull-offs add a smoother sound to the cascading scale.

TRACK 77

EX 179. EXAMPLE IN D MAJOR

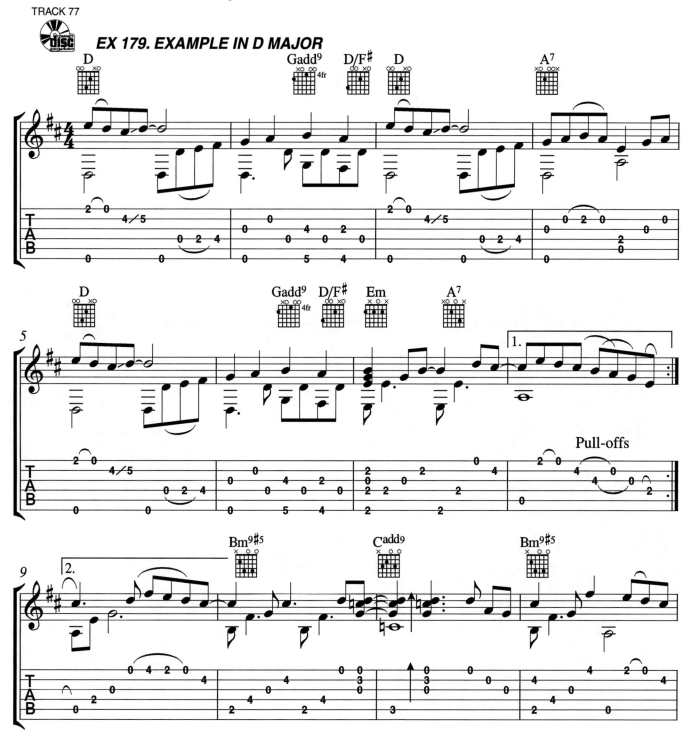

D.C. al Coda

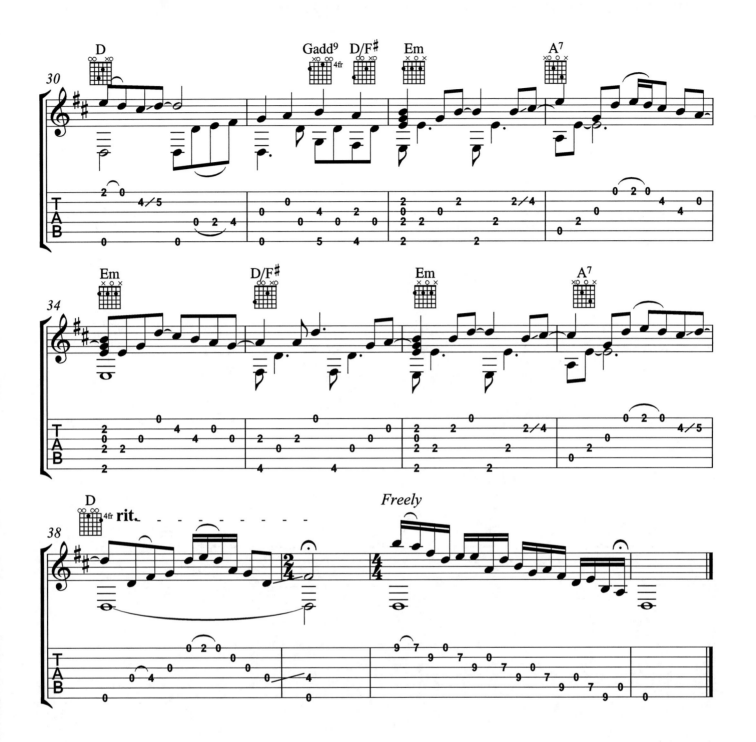

D MINOR

The key of Dm is also a natural key for DADGAD. Depending on the mode in which you are playing, the iv chord may be minor or major (IV) and the v chord may also be minor or major (V) and could also be a dominant seventh.

COMMON CHORDS

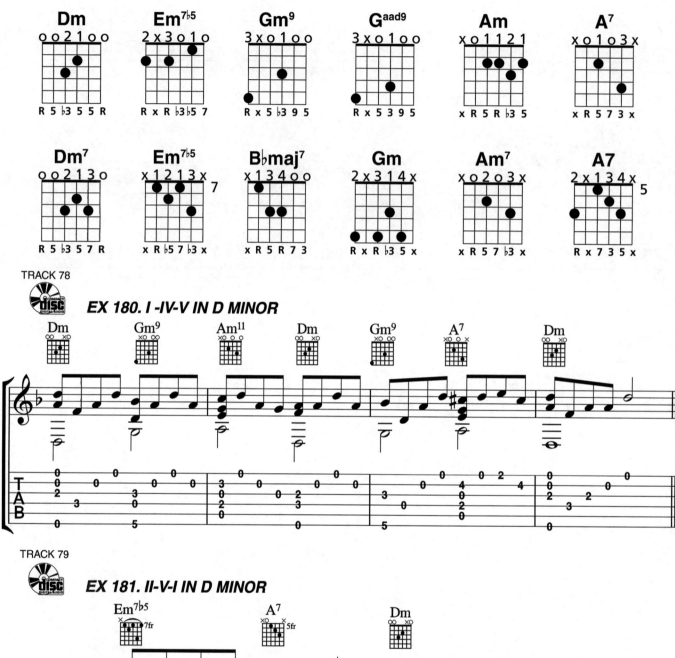

TRACK 78

EX 180. I -IV-V IN D MINOR

TRACK 79

EX 181. II-V-I IN D MINOR

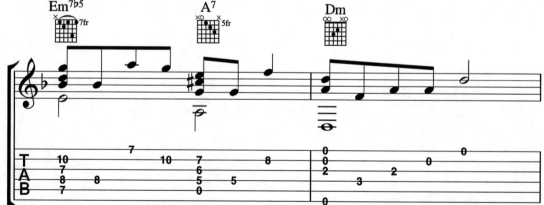

Example 181 provides an example of mixing these modes in a single tune, using both a B♭, which implies the D natural minor, and a B natural, which implies dorian mode.

EX 182. EXAMPLE TUNE IN D MINOR

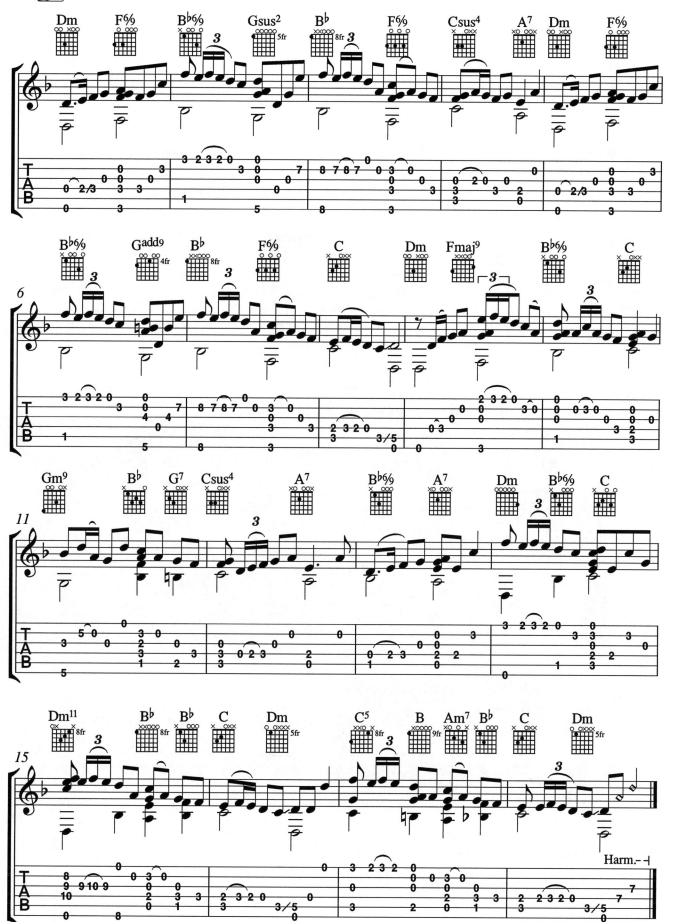

F MAJOR

The key of F is closely related to D minor (D minor is the relative minor of F), so it is no surprise that the key of F works well in DAGDAD. The open D and G strings provide the sixth and ninth relative to F.

COMMON CHORDS

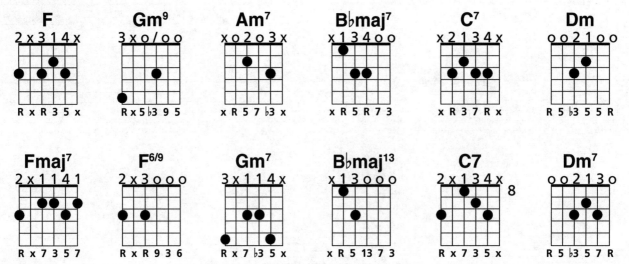

EX 183. A I-IV-V PROGRESSION IN F

TRACK 81

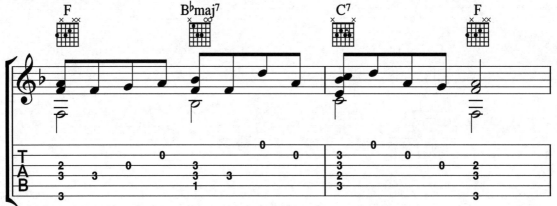

EX 184. A II-V-I PROGRESSION IN F

TRACK 82

Example 185 is an arrangement of the Stephen Foster song, *My Old Kentucky Home*. This tune could be played using only three chords, but this arrangement takes advantage of the rich chords available in DADGAD to introduce more interesting harmonies. Besides using some extended chords, the arrangement often uses chord substitution to enhance the harmony.

TRACK 83

EX 185. MY OLD KENTUCKY HOME, IN THE KEY OF F

127

G MAJOR

Besides D, G is one of the easiest keys to use in DADGAD. The low D works well as the root of the V chord, and all of the main chords in the key are readily accessible.

COMMON CHORDS

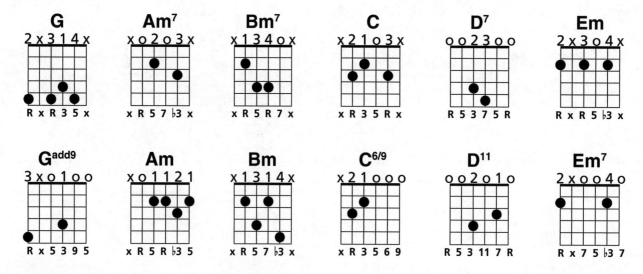

 TRACK 84

EX 186 I-IV-V PROGRESSION IN G

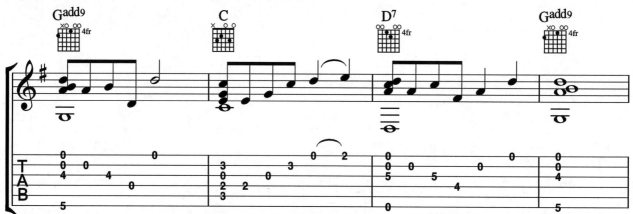

 TRACK 85

EX 187. II-V-I PROGRESSION IN G

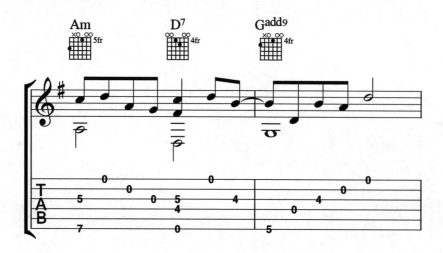

Example 188 is an arrangement of *Twinkle Twinkle Little Star*. The tune starts simply and adds more movement as it proceeds, adding some reharmonization along the way.

TRACK 86

EX 188. TWINKLE TWINKLE LITTLE STAR, IN THE KEY OF G

G MINOR

G minor is a very interesting key in DADGAD. The tension between the B-flat and the open A string creates some colorful chords and unusual melodic opportunities.

COMMON CHORDS

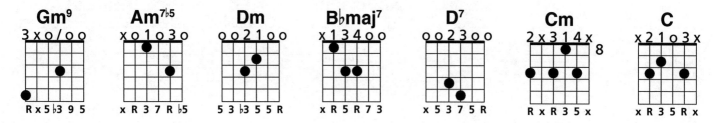

TRACK 87

EX 189. I-IV-V PROGRESSION IN G MINOR

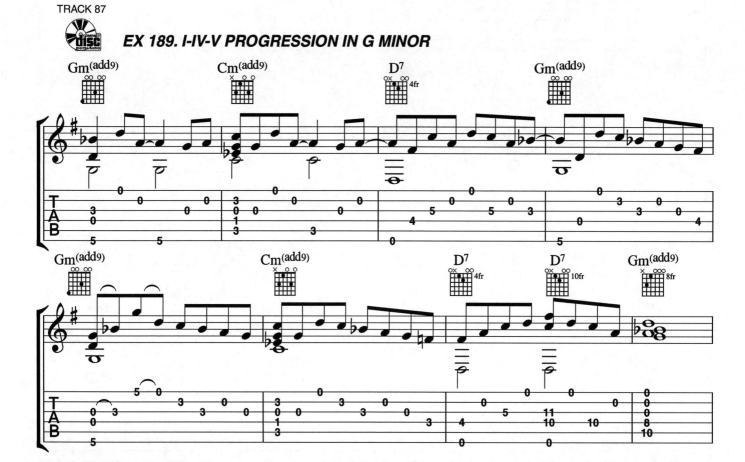

TRACK 88

EX 190. II-V-I PROGRESSION IN G MINOR

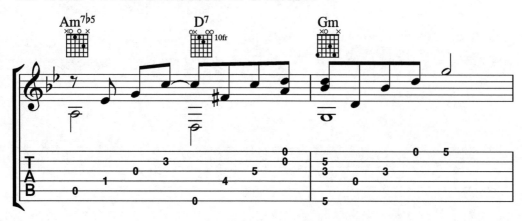

EX 191. EXAMPLE IN G MINOR

A MAJOR

The key of A has quite a bit of potential in DADGAD. There are two open A strings, and the root of the IV chord is available on the lowest string. The root of the V chord (E) is also easily played on the second fret of the sixth string.

COMMON CHORDS

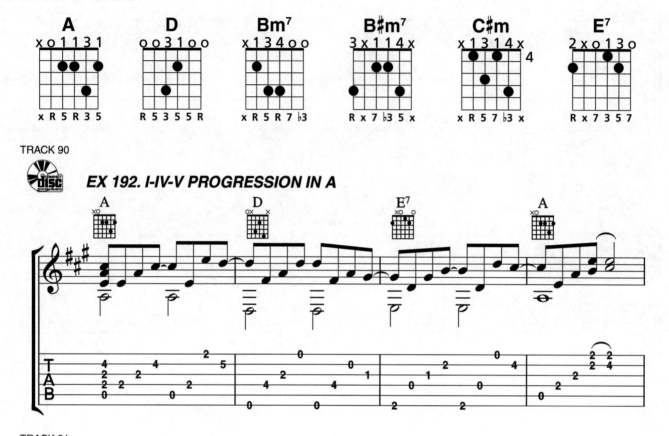

TRACK 90

EX 192. I-IV-V PROGRESSION IN A

TRACK 91

EX 193. II-V-I PROGRESSION IN A

Example 194 is an arrangement of Stephen Foster's *Oh Susanna*. This version uses some cross-string techniques, as well as some chord substitution to enhance the basic three chord harmony of the tune. Notice the B7 in the final verse. This chord, which is not normally found in the key of A, is known as a secondary dominant, because it leads to the dominant seventh chord of the key, an E7.

EX 194. OH SUSANNA IN THE KEY OF A

A MINOR

The key of A minor works well in DADGAD for the same reasons as A major. The fifth string bass note, along with the IV on the sixth string and an assortment of comfortable chord shapes makes the key easy to work with.

COMMON CHORDS

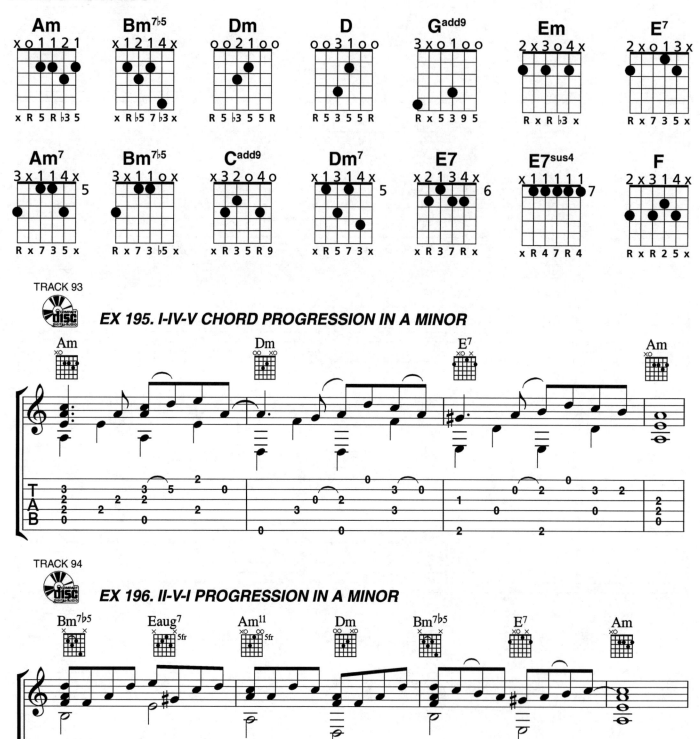

TRACK 93

EX 195. I-IV-V CHORD PROGRESSION IN A MINOR

TRACK 94

EX 196. II-V-I PROGRESSION IN A MINOR

134

Example 197 is an arrangement of the traditional tune, *Greensleeves*. The first verse starts very simply, using mostly first position chords. The second verse, starting at measure 34, introduces a more arpeggiated style, uses more open strings, and also demonstrates some cross-string techniques.

EX 197. GREENSLEEVES, IN A MINOR

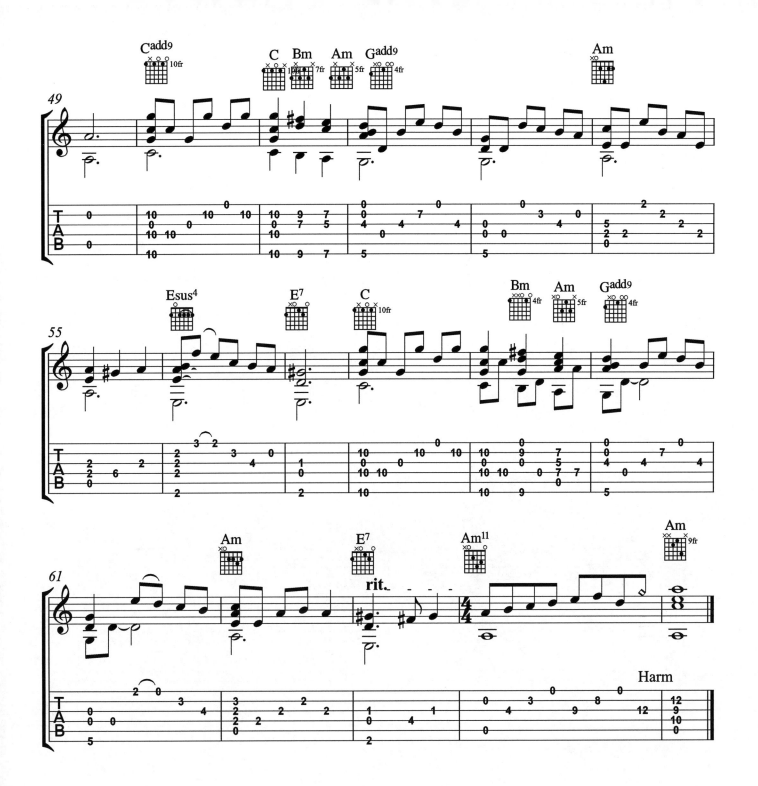

B FLAT MAJOR

The key of B flat is notoriously unfriendly in standard tuning, but works surprisingly well in DADGAD. The open strings form major sevenths with the I and IV chords. The low E-flat on the first fret of the sixth string enables an especially rich IV chord.

COMMON CHORDS

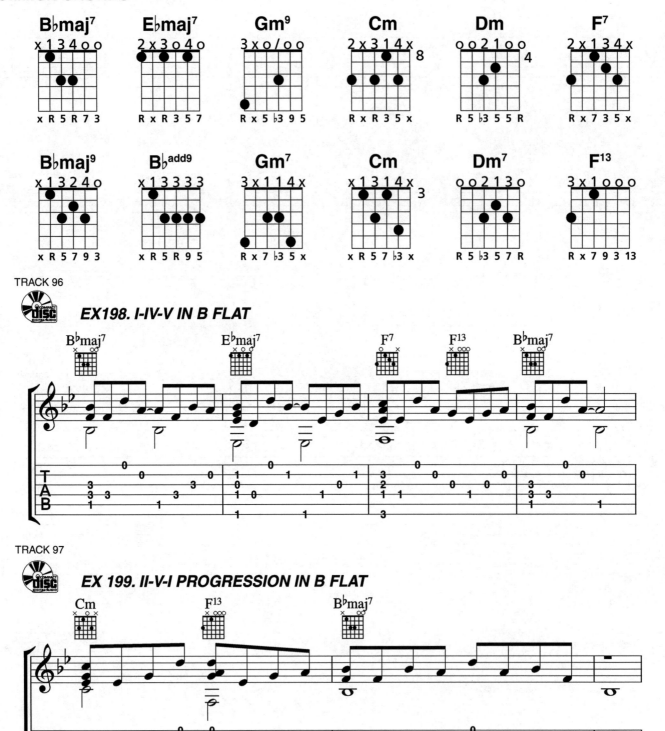

TRACK 96

EX198. I-IV-V IN B FLAT

TRACK 97

EX 199. II-V-I PROGRESSION IN B FLAT

Example 200 leverages the minor ii, iii, and vi chords, as well as major sevenths, ninths, and thirteenths to create a rich sound.

138

EX 200. SWING LOW, SWEET CHARIOT IN B FLAT

NOTES:

NOTES:

NOTES:

NOTES: